WEATHERING MODELS

MAKE ROLLING STOCK, STRUCTURES, AND DETAILS MORE REALISTIC

Jeff Wilson

ACKNOWLEDGMENTS

Thanks to all of the modelers who have inspired me over the years by showing how weathering adds realism to models and scenes: John Allen, Cody Grivno, Tom Johnson, Tony Koester, Keith Kohlmann, Gerry Leone, Allen McClelland, Lance Mindheim, Bob Rivard, Lou Sassi, Jim Six, M.R. Snell, Mont Switzer, George Sellios, Pelle Søeborg, and Michael Tylick, to name just a few. Some of these modelers I've come to know, and many have become friends; others I know only through seeing their modeling in print and online. All, however, have created models and scenes that have inspired me to try techniques and projects. I hope this book does the same for others.

— *Jeff Wilson*

On the cover: Weathering isn't just for freight cars. Along with the rust-streaked boxcar, this HO scale scene is made more realistic by the weathered brick warehouse with its aged, rusted canopy; rusty and grimy vehicles; streets with tar and asphalt patches, streaked with wear patterns; and a stop sign showing rust streaks from mounting bolts and damage.

Opposite page: Basic weathering techniques include paint washes (left), drybrushing and washes over lettering (middle), and stains to age wood (right).

Back cover: Top: A Rock Island steam locomotive shows typical wear, including soot, rust, and general grime, applied with paint, chalks, and PanPastels. **Upper middle:** Along with grime, this automobile has been aged by simulating a missing rear hubcap. **Lower middle:** Real rust adds to the realism of this gondola interior, with oil-paint washes on the sides. **Bottom:** Oil-paint washes add depth to the simulated wood sheathing on a refrigerator car.

All photos by the author unless otherwise credited.

Firecrown
605 Chestnut Street, Suite 800
Chattanooga, TN 37450

Shop.Trains.com

Published in 2024
28 27 26 25 24 1 2 3 4 5

Manufactured in China

ISBN: 979-8-89491-008-6
EISBN: 979-8-89491-009-3

Editor: Steven Otte
Book Design: Lisa Schroeder

CONTENTS

INTRODUCTION

The path toward realistic models

The photo below might seem an odd choice to lead off a book on weathering. After all, it's just an ordinary, nondescript 1950s-era coal-service hopper car. It's dirty and shows some wear, but is obviously still in good physical shape, and has many good years left of hauling coal from mine to customer.

However, that's exactly the point. The major goal in weathering and aging our models is to create the common, everyday appearance of rolling stock, locomotives, structures, vehicles, bridges, and the myriad other details that surround us in the real world.

When some modelers hear the word "weathering," they instantly think of something that's been aged to within an inch of its life, broken and battered and ready to fall apart. Although there are certainly reasons to depict some models to this extent, the idea behind weathering is to provide a variety of appearances that capture the range of objects from brand new to showing some wear to falling apart — and

all points in between. Subtlety is often the key, with varied appearances leading to the best overall results.

For many models, this means simply killing the factory gloss finish and adding a bit of grime. For others, it can mean rust streaks, peeling paint, and weathered wood. Achieving overall realism on a layout comes from blending a mix of all of these effects.

I've found that a good thing about applying weathering effects to models is that it's addictive. Once you do a freight car or two, or perhaps a structure, and see the weathered models standing next to unweathered ones, you'll want to keep going.

Remember that color is the key to producing realistic models. Appropriate colors, finishes, and weathering effects grab viewers' attention more than having exact prototype dimensions or features.

Although this book shows several projects, don't think of it as a project book. My goal throughout is to show a variety of techniques and materials with which I've had success. Try these methods and adapt them to the specific models that you're working on to capture specific prototypes that you want to re-create in miniature.

Not all techniques will work for every modeler. You'll discover that some work better than others, and you'll develop your own favorite tools, materials, and methods. This is fine. If something doesn't work, try something else. The ultimate goal is capturing a realistic appearance, not the technique itself.

Also, keep in mind that specific models go in and out of production frequently. Some models and materials shown in this book may not be made any more. I've tried to indicate alternatives in many cases. Always check eBay and other online sites for discontinued models. If something has been offered in the past, it's likely available somewhere on the internet.

For now, choose a project and dive in. Once you get started, you'll find more and more models to work on, and you'll gain the confidence to keep trying new techniques.

The weathering on this HO scale Accurail two-bay hopper is simple — some drybrushed black streaks over the lettering to simulate peeling paint, a bit of powdered-chalk grime on the sides, and detail painting on the trucks.

CHAPTER ONE

Weathering basics

Weathering is more than a handy set of techniques for making your models look grimy. It's what turns toys and toy-like miniatures into realistic scale models. Sound extreme? Perhaps, but it's accurate. Weathering is simply the most effective thing you can do to improve the appearance of a model or scene.

This applies to models of all types, not just cars and locomotives. Structures, vehicles, streets, signs, track, and other details will all be improved by making them look like they've been out in the real world.

A superbly modeled scene without a bit of weathering — even if the modeling is first-rate and prototypical to the scale inch — will stand out as a model and look toylike if the finish is glossy and bright and everything looks new.

As Lance Mindheim — one of the best modelers in the hobby today — so aptly pointed out in his book *Modeling Structures*, color and finish are the Nos. 1 and 2 keys to realistic appearance. This applies to all models, not just buildings. Not accurate dimensions, nor whether a boxcar has a Miner brake wheel instead of an Ajax version. The color and weathering treatment you apply to models matters!

WEATHERING GOALS

"Weathering" is a broad term. The basic idea is that we're trying to capture in a realistic manner the color and finish characteristics of objects in the real world, whether it be a boxcar, locomotive, structure, or vehicle.

Look around as you go for a walk or a drive and you will see objects in a wide variety of states of cleanliness and repair, from brand new to slightly worn to ramshackle and weatherbeaten. Every object that we see is on a journey from new/factory fresh to old and about to be retired/scrapped/thrown away. It's our task as modelers to figure out where on that journey we want to capture the appearance of each car, locomotive, or other feature.

If everything on your layout is weathered to within an inch of its life, the effect — even if you're modeling a period during the Depression — won't be realistic. A blend of old and new, with appropriate selections, should be the goal.

Our aim as modelers is usually to strive to capture the feel of the particular railroad or city we're modeling, in a specific era, or if freelancing, to capture a place and point in time. For example, if you're modeling 1971, a boxcar built in 1970 should look new and in good shape; a boxcar built in 1960 will likely be grimy and showing wear, and one built in 1950 would have significant weathering and possibly some rust.

Another key is to find and develop the weathering techniques and materials that work best for you. There are tons of products available and many ways of applying them. We'll cover

Union Pacific 2-10-2 No. 5015 rolls a long string of Pacific Fruit Express refrigerator cars across Nebraska in the 1950s. The cars all started as the same color, but weathering has given each a unique appearance. New and freshly painted equipment, like the car behind the engine, stands out among cars that have been in service for several years. Linn Westcott

Cody Grivno used artist's oils, cosmetic applicators, and an airbrush with thinned acrylic paints to create this HO model of a well-traveled former Berlin Mills Ry. boxcar. Its prototype was built in 1979; the model represents the car a few decades later when it was owned by the Green Mountain RR. Firecrown Media

many in this book, but understand that some will work better for you than others. That's OK! If you try a technique or type of paint that just doesn't work, skip it and try something else.

Like other modelers, I've come to rely on certain methods as my "go-to" techniques, and there are others that just don't work well for me, even though they provide beautiful results for other modelers.

Always, always test paint and methods before applying them to your prize models. I keep scrap materials and old car shells handy for this. And be aware that like any motor skill, it can take a few tries to master and become comfortable with many techniques.

This book is not meant to be all-encompassing. There are other techniques out there, and space precludes showing examples of every type of rolling stock or structure. The examples throughout this book, including my own and those done by other skilled modelers, are designed to give you a broad overview and help inspire you to develop ideas for your own models.

KEY TO REALISM: FLAT FINISH

Few things kill the effect of otherwise realistic models on a layout like glossy finishes. If you do nothing else to your models, give them a coat of clear flat finish. This applies to virtually everything: freight cars, locomotives, vehicles, structures, and details. About the only exceptions are window glazing and other "glass" details.

"But," I can almost hear you say, "lots of things in real life are shiny! I just saw a new auto/freight car/locomotive up close, and it was glossy! And you just told me that we should have a mix of things that look new as well as old! What gives?"

The basic reasons are scale and distance: A new automobile with a waxed, buffed finish looks great in your driveway, but an HO or N scale model with the same shiny finish will look toylike under most lighting situations on our layouts.

Artificial light highlights things differently in miniature than the sun does to full-size objects, including the way it creates shadows and contrast, how

Learning how and why prototype equipment weathers the way it does is the key to capturing it on a model. Left: This Burlington Northern boxcar has rust patches near the roofline; Mother Nature has washed rust stains down the sides, streaking the lettering and painted side. There are numerous methods of re-creating weathering effects. Right: One effective method of modeling downward rust streaks is with artist's oil colors washed downward with a turpentine-soaked brush, as on this HO gondola.

it affects color, and in the amount of light that's needed to see details.

A caveat is that this effect might not be apparent in all situations. The HO boxcar and refrigerator cars on pages 10 and 11 highlight this — both have been given a brush-coat of acrylic clear flat finish. As is, both will look great in some lighting, but if the light catches it a certain way, the lettering vanishes and the color fades, as shown on the refrigerator car.

The lettering on the Milwaukee Road car (which on most models is ink, not paint) is the main culprit on that model, as it's glossy, killing the realism. Fixing it was a simple matter of applying a clear flat coat.

Glossy models on a layout will continually pick up and reflect light when we don't want them to: a gray plastic roadway that you suddenly notice reflects the ceiling lights, a brick building with a shiny spot in the middle of a wall where it reflects a streetlight, and so on.

The other important reason to add a flat finish to models is that it makes all future weathering methods more effective, whether you're using chalks,

Every piece of equipment you see is at some point on its journey from brand new to retired, and its appearance will reflect where on that spectrum it resides. The top image shows a Sabine River & Northern boxcar a year after it was built in 1976, still looking new in its bright red scheme. By 2004, a sister car — now 28 years old and owned by H&S RR Co. — is showing its age with well-worn, darkened paint; faded lettering; graffiti; and many dings, scrapes, and rust spots. Top: J. David Ingles; Bottom: Jeff Wilson

Most factory-decorated models come in semigloss or gloss finishes. Top: Adding a clear coat of flat finish is easy with an airbrush, spray can, or brush (here using the now-discontinued Polly Scale clear flat finish). Bottom: The difference in finish is striking, especially when light catches a model's surface. The bright reflection at left is distracting; the flat finish applied on the right side minimizes glare and provides a more realistic appearance.

artist's pencils, thinned-paint washes, drybrushing, or other techniques. It's almost impossible to make chalk and paint washes stick to glossy surfaces. Applying a dead-flat finish solves that problem.

DARK COLORS VANISH

An important thing in determining what colors to use when weathering and painting details is that dark colors (particularly black, Brunswick Green, and dark blue) make details disappear under typical layout lighting. Look at the black trucks on a typical ready-to-run diesel locomotive model. Or, heaven forbid, a steam locomotive model painted pure black. There simply isn't enough light in a basement or layout room to penetrate these dark colors to bring out details.

The solution to this problem is twofold. First: Never paint anything on a model pure black. It doesn't matter if the prototype was black or not. Start with dark gray (usually called "grimy black" by paint manufacturers) and test it. Ditto for other dark colors: Lighten them with a bit of white if you're painting a model from the start.

(You can use this to your advantage in some cases. If you have something you want to make disappear visually — such as part of an unrealistic frame behind a locomotive truck — paint it flat black.)

For models already painted in these dark colors, weathering provides the key, as we'll see in the following chapters. Applying a flat finish to the model, then following with lighter-colored weathering to simulate grime, rust, dust, and sand, will lighten the overall shade and make details stand out and appear more realistic.

FOLLOW THE PROTOTYPE

Many modelers take the first step toward realistic weathering by broadly applying chalks or weathering sprays to all of the cars in their fleet. This is certainly better than glossy painted roofs; however, a generic approach doesn't really duplicate how objects in the real world get their aged appearances.

For example, automatically giving all your freight cars' roofs a heavy overspray or wash of sooty grimy black and dirt misses the point that roofs are generally fairly clean. Rain drives against horizontal flat surfaces much harder than vertical car sides, keeping the roofs free of much grime. Roofs do, however, rust in various patterns (depending upon the type of roof and material used), and colors tend to bleach and fade more heavily because the sun's rays strike roofs more directly than car sides.

Train yourself to observe what's actually there, not what you think you see or have seen. For example: What color is galvanized metal (as on many boxcar roofs)? Many simply say "silver" (and that's what model manufacturers often use). The truth is that it's really a dull, metallic gray.

The best advice I've received from veteran modelers — and that I pass along to others — is to study specific prototype examples and then determine the best weathering materials and techniques to duplicate them in miniature. Fortunately there's a wealth of resources available to us for prototype information, in the form of websites and color-photograph books.

Starting in the next chapter we'll look at various paints, chalks, and other materials available to us. We'll follow that with application techniques such as washes, drybrushing, and oversprays. Building a repertoire of these will help give you create a wide variety of effects, including rust, grime, soot, and stains from loads.

HOW MUCH IS TOO MUCH?

How much time you take with each model — and the amount and detail of weathering on each — is certainly a matter of personal taste and preference. Do you have a small shelf layout with about 20 to 30 pieces of rolling stock and three locomotives? Then you can probably afford to spend a lot of time with each individual model to get the effects just right. Or are you working on a basement empire with a couple hundred freight cars? Then it's likely you'll be making a "quick pass" approach on many cars.

A common way to look at it when starting with a project is asking yourself if it is a "one-foot model" or a "four-foot model." In other words, will it frequently be getting close-up scrutiny from close range? Or will it be rolling in a train with a bunch of other cars, with viewers merely catching the overall effects from several feet away?

Lighting is a factor, as well. As you're weathering a model, take it to your layout so you can evaluate it in the lighting where it will most often be seen. You might look at a model under a bright workbench light and think that it needs another layer of grime, but moving it under (usually) dimmer layout lighting can show that it's already heavier than you'd planned.

As you go through of the chapters and projects throughout this book, work on developing ideas for your own projects. By all means base your models on your favorite prototypes and use the materials and techniques that work best for you.

The paint on this HO boxcar is actually matte; however, the lettering is glossy — a common problem, as many manufacturers use ink instead of paint for lettering. The four body panels at right have been brushed with acrylic clear flat finish, eliminating the shine.

Basic weathering effects

Flat finish plus thinned black wash

Clear flat finish applied

Original silver paint

Weathering doesn't have to be heavy to be effective. As an example, many boxcar models come with silver roofs, which are too bright to accurately represent the dull metallic gray of galvanized steel. At right is the boxcar's original silver roof; the middle section shows how a simple clear flat coat toned down the silver. A wash of thinned black acrylic (left) greatly improved the effect, even on what is supposed to be a fairly new car.

CHAPTER TWO

You can use any number of materials for weathering, including acrylic and oil paints, powdered and solid chalks, paint markers, and pencils.

Paint, chalk, brushes, and tools

We have a tremendous variety of materials at our disposal to create weathering effects. Whether to use paints, chalks, pencils, markers, or other materials, or a combination of them — and how to apply them — is largely a matter of personal comfort and taste, as there are many ways to get realistic weathered finishes on models.

Keep in mind that the color itself is the most important characteristic, regardless of whether we're dealing with paint, chalk, or another medium. Model paint manufacturers name their paint for specific weathering effects: grimy black, dark rust, roof brown, etc. These names can be handy as a starting point, but pay more attention to the color than the name. For example, one of my most-used rust colors is a craft paint named "espresso," which has a great dark-brown color.

In this chapter we'll take a look at the many types of paint, chalk, and other products available and examine their properties. We'll then take a look at brushes and other tools. In Chapter 3 we'll start looking at the many types of weathering techniques. Let's start with a look at paint.

I prefer acrylics for most modeling, including standard modeling paints (Polly Scale at left and Vallejo at right) as well as craft paints. Artist's oil colors (in tubes) are handy for rust and other effects.

PAINT FINISH AND TYPE

Many types and brands of paints will produce excellent effects on our models, including conventional modeling paints, craft paints, and artist's acrylic and oil paints. What you choose to use is largely a matter of personal taste. There are a couple of key points to consider regarding finish and paint formula.

The first is the finish, or sheen. On our models, as Chapter 1 explained, we almost always want paint that has a dead-flat finish. A lot of model paints, especially those made as specific railroad colors, are made in gloss or semi-glass (to provide a smooth surface for decal application). Weathering colors in model paint lines, however, are generally flat. Acrylic craft paint is available in either flat or gloss finish. Check labels carefully and make sure you're using the flat versions.

ACRYLICS VS. SOLVENTS

The second key property is the paint's solvent or carrier base. There are two basic types: acrylics, which are water based, and solvent-based paints (lacquers and enamels), which use organic solvents such as lacquer thinner or mineral spirits as a base.

Into the 1990s, most modeling paints (primarily the Floquil and Scalecoat brands) were lacquers or

A clear flat finish is vital for realism and to provide a base for weathering effects. From left are Model Master and Polly Scale clear flats, Krylon matte and gloss finish in spray cans, and acrylic matte medium.

Powdered chalk is available from several sources; these are from AIM Products (now Monroe Models). Artist's pastel chalks are quite handy, as is mica-free makeup (right).

enamels. The emergence of better-performing, improved-formula acrylics such as Floquil's Polly Scale and Badger's Modelflex, plus the eventual discontinuance of several earlier paint brands, has led to much greater popularity of acrylics.

Current modeling-specific acrylic offerings include Modelflex, Vallejo, Rail Center, and Tamiya; there are others, as well. Polly Scale and other paints are still available from some sources even though they've been discontinued by their manufacturers.

Over the past 20 years, I have come to use acrylic paints almost exclusively. They are easy to use, work well, bond firmly to surfaces, and clean up easily and safely with water. There are none of the hassles and hazards of using lacquer thinner and other solvents to clean brushes or airbrushes, and no dangerous solvent vapors to deal with.

You'll thus find acrylics used almost exclusively throughout this book. If you choose to use solvent-based paints, most of the same techniques apply, but you'll be using the paint's recommended thinner in place of water or alcohol-based thinners. Be aware of the dangers of these chemicals and only use them with adequate ventilation.

My two exceptions to this are artist's oil colors, which use turpentine as a cleaner and solvent, and clear finish from a spray can, which we'll cover in a moment.

PAINTING TIPS

- Give all models a clear flat finish before adding weathering effects.
- Always test for compatibility before mixing paints with each other or with a nonstandard thinner.
- Test for compatibility when applying dissimilar paint types (including washes) over each other.
- If a clear finish turns foggy or milky, it can usually be fixed by applying a coat of clear gloss and starting over.
- Keep threads of paint bottles and lids clean.
- If a bottle of paint has started to go bad (globs or dried paint that won't mix or dissolve), throw it away.
- Use good-quality brushes and clean them thoroughly after each use.

WORKING WITH PAINT

To thin acrylics (for creating washes or for airbrushing), you can use water; however, the surface tension will cause thin mixes to bead up when they're applied. A better choice (if you're thinning paint more than 30 percent or so) is an alcohol-based thinner. All acrylic brands offer their own lines of thinner; another popular choice among modelers is automotive windshield washer solution (the blue kind). The surface tension of the alcohol is much lower

Pastel chalk sticks can be scraped with a hobby knife to create powder; powders can be mixed to create a variety of colors.

PanPastels — pigment in cake form — are available in a tremendous variety of colors. They can be applied with a makeup sponge (shown) or brush.

than water, allowing washes and oversprays to be applied in very thin coats without beading up.

And yes, the alcohol thinners do require care in using. Avoid breathing the vapors, especially if airbrushing. I strongly recommend working in a vented spray booth.

Any time you opt for a non-standard thinner, test the mix first to make sure the paint doesn't react (curdling or turning chalky are common reactions). Also, mix only as much as you plan to use in a session. Thinned paint tends to separate over time.

Always test paints when applying one type of paint over another, as unintended reactions can sometimes occur, including cracking and discoloration. An example: applying acrylic thinned with alcohol over Testor's Dullcote (and some other clear finishes) will result in a lightened, frosted effect. This can be used to our benefit if we know what's going to happen, but you don't want to be surprised by a reaction.

Artist's oil (tube) paints have become popular for weathering. For our purposes, a little oil paint goes a long way, so buy small tubes. Turpentine is preferred for thinning the paint, creating washes, and cleaning brushes and paint cups. Turpentine substitute is also available. I use Turpenoid, an odorless product that works well (but as it's a petroleum distillate, it still requires care in handling).

If you choose to use lacquers or enamels, always use them in a well-ventilated area. If you airbrush them, only do so outdoors or in a vented spray booth and wear a respirator-style mask and nitrile gloves.

KEEPING PAINT FRESH

Regardless of the paint type, there are a few tricks that will keep them fresh and extend their shelf lives. A knock against acrylics is that sometimes seem to dry up or solidify in the bottle faster than solvent-based paints. But thanks to some care, I have bottles of Polly Scale and Modelflex that are more than 20 years old that are still in great shape.

First, remember that air is the enemy of small bottles of paint — especially acrylics. If you open a bottle, get it closed as soon as possible so it doesn't stand open on your workbench

From the top are paint markers, artist's pencils, and pastel crayons (which have been shaped to fine points).

any longer than necessary. If you're doing a project where you'll be spending 15 minutes brushing a color, use a pipette to transfer paint to a tray so you can close the bottle.

If paint gets on the threads of the bottle or cap, wipe it off before closing the bottle. This paint will dry, making it tough to open the bottle, and the subsequent dried bits will contaminate the paint in the bottle. If you open a bottle and find a film has formed over the top, remove it with tweezers and clean the bottle and cap threads.

CLEAR FINISHES

Throughout this book you'll see an emphasis on clear, flat finishes on models. Getting this can be done in a number of ways. My preferred method is acrylic flat clear, applied with a brush or airbrush (Tamiya and Model Master both offer this, and both have acrylic thinners, as well). Although it's no longer produced, I still have a stock of Polly Scale clear acrylic, which I've used with success thinning with Polly S airbrush thinner or common windshield washer solution.

I always thin clear flat, even when brushing it, as not doing so can result in a slightly white, milky, or foggy appearance and a tendency to show brush strokes. For brushing, I start with a mix of roughly 60% flat and 40% thinner; for airbrushing, it's closer to 50/50. Humidity, temperature, and other factors can influence results, so experiment a bit to find what works for you.

For speed and ease of application, the classic spray can is sometimes a good option for clear finishes. Spray finishes are quick, without the cleanup required by an airbrush. My favorites are Krylon's Matte Finish (flat) and, if you need a gloss finish for decaling, Crystal Clear (gloss). Although Testor's Dullcote has been around for decades and is a staple for many modelers, I've never had success getting an even finish with it. Your mileage may vary: find a product that works for you and stick with it.

The biggest challenge is that clear finishes in spray cans involve multiple ingredients that are hazardous to breathe. Don't use spray cans indoors unless you have a vented spray booth.

A related product is acrylic matte medium. It looks and acts like white glue, but dries clear with a flat finish. Later chapters show how I use it as a base for mixing with chalk and real rust, as well as using it as an adhesive.

CHALK, MAKEUP, PANPASTELS

Chalks are extremely versatile for weathering and creating various effects, and they're available in several forms. Perhaps the handiest are powdered chalks made in specific weathering colors, available from AIM Products (now owned by Monroe Models), Bar Mills, Bragdon Enterprises, Micro-Mark, and others.

Colors vary in name, so look at the actual colors: they include black and various shades of gray, buff, and brown to simulate rust, dirt, grime, and soot. Powdered chalks are also easily blended to create additional color shades.

Artists' pastel chalks are also a great resource. They come in sticks, again in various colors. I keep a set of gray and brown chalks handy. They can be used by applying them directly or by making powder by scraping them with a hobby knife. (Avoid kids' toy or playground

PAINTBRUSH CARE

- Wet the brush before painting, then pull it through a paper towel. This will help keep paint from drying on the bristles.
- Never leave a brush sitting in a jar of thinner. The bristles will become bent and distorted.
- Only dip the bristle tips into paint. Keep the paint out of the ferrule (the metal band that holds the bristles).
- Store brushes bristles up/handle down in a cup or storage rack.
- Always clean brushes immediately after using.
- If a brush becomes damaged or starts to lose its shape, remove it from primary service and keep it for other uses, such as drybrushing, applying chalk, or applying glue.

Soft, wide, flat-bristle brushes (the three at left) are great for applying washes. Small round-tip brushes (the Nos. 2 and 0 brushes at right) are good for fine details. The third brush from right is a stiff (hog-bristle) brush, handy for grinding chalk into surfaces.

Airbrushes are handy for creating many weathering effects, such as the grimy coat on this tank car. The thinned paint is being applied with a basic Paasche H single-action airbrush.

Aluminum trays work well for mixing and holding small amounts of paint. Other handy items include toothpicks of various sizes, cotton swabs, makeup sponges, and small jars and containers. Don't try to pour paint from small bottles. Instead, use pipettes and eyedroppers. Be sure to keep them clean.

INDIA INK WASHES

Many modelers use a wash of India ink mixed with common (70%) rubbing alcohol for weathering. If you try this, aim for a thinner mix than with paint: typically closer to 5% ink and 95% alcohol, but you can adjust the percentages based on results. The basic purpose is to provide an overall cast of grime and add contrast, similar to a thinned black paint wash. You can mix the wash in the alcohol bottle itself or another small container, and the mix will stay good for a long time.

Although I use ink washes for staining wood, I typically rely on thinned paint washes for most other purposes. I've found paint easier to control and adjust — but this is just my personal preference. Give India ink washes a try and evaluate their effectiveness yourself.

chalks, which won't adhere as well.)

Chalks usually require a clear overcoat to hold them in place, especially on models that will be handled (such as freight cars); we don't want fingerprints to show. The clear finish can sometimes diminish the chalk effect. Test to see the effects.

Related to chalk is fashion makeup such as eye shadow and other powdered materials. These come in handy flip-lid cases in a variety of colors, including a wide range of reds, browns, and grays. If you decide to try makeup, be sure to get a mica-free brand (mica is the sparkly material that gives sheen to a lot of makeup materials, which is not something we want for our models). Although makeup is more expensive than other chalks, an advantage is that it is made to stick. It holds up well on surfaces and the colors won't fade or disappear when clear coated.

PanPastels are artists' pastel paints that come in cake form. Their consistency is soft, but with more body than chalk. Application is usually with makeup sponges or small brushes. They bond well to surfaces and are available in a wide range of colors, including browns and grays that are ideal for weathering. They're extremely versatile and have become one of my main go-to materials for weathering.

MARKERS AND PENCILS

Paint markers look like permanent markers, but deliver paint (usually enamel) instead of ink from their felt tips. Model paint manufacturers have offered several of these in colors useful for weathering such as browns and dark reds. Sharpie (which also makes permanent markers) offers several colors of paint markers.

Permanent markers use ink instead of paint. Be aware that their ink, which is usually alcohol-based, can react to some clear overcoats and other paints.

Artists' pencils are handy in reds, grays, blacks, and browns. They're great for highlighting small details and applying rust, grime, and other colors to specific areas and components. They adhere well and have softer lead than children's colored pencils. White pencils can be used to simulate chalk marks on cars.

Pastel crayons are a cross between an artist's pencil and chalk. Their ends can be shaved or filed to a point, allowing fine control of adding color to small details and areas.

A key is that all of these materials should be applied to dead-flat finishes; they will not adhere well to glossy or semi-gloss surfaces.

"REAL" MATERIALS

In addition to paints, chalks, and other materials that simulate prototype effects, you may find a use in modeling to use materials from nature or actual products in loads. Examples include actual rust, either in pieces or ground to a powder (see Chapter 6), as well as various types of dirt, soil, and sand, again usually in fine powdered form. Chapter 6 shows an example of using actual cement to model a cement spill atop a covered hopper.

Be aware that this is a hit-and-miss process, as the appearance of some real materials won't scale down well to our modeled sizes. Any kind of dirt or soil will need to be screened and sifted to get the proper sizes, and won't easily adhere to model surfaces as well as paint or chalk does.

Don't do this with materials that are potentially hazardous, and always take care in preparing and sealing these materials.

BRUSHES

Paintbrushes are a key tool in applying weathering effects, including washes, drybrushing, and applying chalk. My first key piece of advice with brushes: Don't skimp. You don't need the finest art-quality brushes, but spend a few dollars for high-quality items. Good brushes will apply paint more smoothly, will clean more readily, won't shed bristles, will last longer, and will be a pleasure to use.

The photo on page 16 shows the brushes I use most often. Flat, soft-bristle artist's brushes in ¼", ⅜", ½", ¾", and 1" widths are great for applying washes and general painting needs. Smaller round-tip brushes work well for getting paint into tight areas and weathering intricate details. For drybrushing and working with some chalk effects, I have a few stiff-bristle (usually hog-bristle) brushes.

My second piece of advice with brushes: Take care of them! High-quality brushes will last a long time and work much better if you clean them thoroughly and often.

Use the appropriate cleaner for

SAND

the type of paint you use. Since I use acrylics almost exclusively, this makes cleaning simple with water and — at the end of each modeling session — dish soap. I keep a cup of water at my workbench to quickly clean brushes between paint coats or quick color changes. Do this immediately: swish the brush repeatedly in the water, then pull it through a paper towel, reshaping the bristles as you do so.

At the end of the day (or the painting session), take your brushes to a utility sink. Under running water, place a drop of soap on the bristles and work it in with your fingers. Then, rinse the bristles thoroughly.

If you've used a lacquer, enamel, or oil paint, swish the brush in the appropriate thinner (lacquer thinner or mineral spirits), then pull it through a paper towel. Repeat until it's clean, then follow by washing it with soap and water.

Instead of a brush, you can use a cotton swab for many quick-use weathering applications where precision isn't needed. Makeup application sponges are also handy for many situations with chalk, PanPastels, and paint.

AIRBRUSHING

An airbrush is not a necessary tool, but it will certainly come in handy if you do a lot of weathering and painting. They're handy for creating subtle weathering effects.

I wouldn't buy one just to weather a handful of freight cars, but if you do a lot of painting and weathering, you'll find it a worthwhile investment. And an investment it is, as you not only need the airbrush itself, but a compressor or other source of air, as well as a spray booth to safely use it indoors. Details on airbrushes and airbrushing are beyond the scope of this book, but you have many options available from companies like Badger, Binks, Iwata, and Paasche.

MISCELLANEOUS TOOLS

Small aluminum paint trays with multiple recessed cups are handy for holding small amounts of paint to keep from having bottles open for long periods. Paint can be mixed in these trays, and you can easily mix small batches of washes while adjusting the amount of paint and thinner. Be sure to clean them immediately after using.

For paint mixes and washes that you want to save for another session, you'll need small jars or cups with replaceable airtight caps. Along with paint mixes or washes, these work well for holding chalk, dirt, sand, and other materials. They're available from craft stores and hobby shops.

Pouring paint from a small bottle rarely goes well. Instead, transfer paint and thinner with eyedroppers and pipettes. They work well and are easy to clean (use a pipe cleaner with water or thinner).

Toothpicks are versatile. They work well for mixing paint and for moving paint a drop at a time. They also work well for applying small dabs and dots of paint precisely, for rubbing against the edges of masking tape to seal it, and to remove small bits of unwanted weathering paint (rubbing a toothpick on the surface usually won't damage the underlying surface or base paint). I keep them handy at my workbench in a variety of sizes.

CHAPTER THREE

Weathering techniques and methods

Chapter 2 showed our basic weathering materials. Now how do we best apply them to models? There are a number of techniques, including washes, drybrushing, and dusting, each of which has many variations in application. The key to keep in mind is to do whatever best replicates the prototype effect you're trying to capture.

Washes are just one of the many common weathering methods that are easy to learn and use. This wash, made with artist's oil paint and turpentine, is settling into the grooves, highlighting the texture of this simulated wood-side refrigerator car.

For an oil-paint wash, load the brush with turpentine, then touch it to the desired color paint. Add more thinner if the initial effect is too heavy.

We'll look at a number of different techniques, starting with paint and moving to chalk and other materials. In many cases you'll find that to capture a specific prototype effect requires combining techniques; for example, using a paint wash followed by a chalk application.

Many weathering effects are best done in layers. A good piece of advice is to always start out light and build up effects slowly. If you start with a light touch, you can always make it darker; however, if you start with a too-heavy effect, you might not be able to reverse the process.

You'll also learn that some techniques are very forgiving and easy to correct if they don't come out right the first time, while others give you one chance to get it right (or a very limited working time before they become permanent).

As you weather any given model, pause and give it a good look under bright lighting to see if the effect is truly what you're looking for; compare it to a photo if possible. I sometimes find it helpful to set a model aside for a day or two between weathering layers. This provides a fresh look to critically see effects.

Let's start with some effects using various types of paint.

WASHES

A wash is simply a thinned mix of paint, applied with a brush. Washes tend to settle in cracks and crevices; they highlight details with complex shapes; they can simulate an overall layer of grime over a surface; and they add contrast by simulating shadows, as they tend to collect around raised details such as rivets and weld seams.

Specific mixes for washes vary depending on the effect you're looking for. A good starting point is about 10% paint and 90% thinner; you can then test and adjust as needed. Another quick way to do a wash is to place some paint on a card or piece of scrap plastic, then wet the brush in water (or thinner) and touch it to the paint. Practice to see the effects.

With acrylics, your choice of thinner greatly affects what a wash will do. If you use water, the wash will tend to bead up on the surface and not penetrate into cracks and crevices. (This can be a strength or weakness, as well see in projects throughout this book.)

My usual choice is either the paint's specific thinner (for model paints) or common windshield-washer fluid (the blue kind) for craft paints. Always test before using on a real model. Because alcohol has a much lower surface tension than water, it will easily flow into and penetrate tight spaces and gaps.

Washes work best for large textured areas, such as the sides of wood-sheathed freight cars, as well as freight-car roofs, ends, and doors. They also work well for many structure surfaces, such as brick, corrugated steel, clapboard, and many types of roofing.

Washes are also handy where simulated depth is needed, such as grills and screens on diesel locomotives, as well as providing contrast and highlighting detail on small textured details and surfaces.

Washes don't always work well on large, smooth surfaces. They can tend to pool and swirl, creating unrealistic, unintended effects (see "Correcting a bad wash effect" on page 25).

To avoid beading, washes are best applied to a dead-flat finish. If your model has a glossy surface, give it a coat of clear flat finish before applying the wash.

MIXING AND APPLYING WASHES

If I'm weathering a bunch of models at once, or if I know I'll be doing more models within a few days, I'll mix a wash in a small resealable bottle. If I'm just doing a single model, I simply mix the wash in a small paint tray.

Many colors can work for washes. Most common for grime effects are various shades of medium to dark gray and black. My go-to is simply flat acrylic craft paint, starting with a drop of black and a drop or two of medium or dark gray, or a drop of brown.

For more rusted effects, start with dark brown, adding drops of medium brown or ochre. For sand or buff effects, start with a tan or buff yellow color, mixing in light gray or white.

Always test the wash on a small area to make sure the color and shade are what you're looking for. Keep in mind that the wash will usually lighten as it dries.

For large surfaces, apply the wash with a flat, soft-bristle brush. Use as

Acrylic paint/alcohol washes settle in low-relief details, making them ideal for adding depth to features such as diesel locomotive grills.

You can use the high surface tension property of a water-based wash on elevated details by placing the wash on the detail, like this hinge. Surface tension will keep the color on the detail only, so it won't flow over the edge.

wide a brush as is practical. In most cases, such as the sides and roofs of freight cars, we want to duplicate the effects of Mother Nature, which washes things downward. Do this with the brush, stroking downward and following details such as weld seams and rivet lines.

Keep an eye on the wash as it dries, making sure no unrealistic pooling occurs (especially on smooth areas). A brush with water or thinner will take care of this, or a dry brush if the wash was simply too heavy.

Once a wash dries, you can add a second coat, or add another wash of a different color (brown over dark gray, for example).

Another technique where water-based washes can be effective is for details that are elevated above surrounding surfaces. The photos below left show this with the hinges on a refrigerator car. By applying a water-based wash, the surface tension of the water keeps it from running over the edge. When it dries, only the hinge will carry the paint effects.

The following chapters include several examples of using washes.

OIL-PAINT WASHES

Artist's oil colors have become very popular with modelers in the past couple of decades. They're effective at adding grime and rust effects on large, smooth surfaces (such as steel freight car sides) where acrylic washes tend to pool and form unrealistic patterns.

I find that Mars black and a collection of three browns — burnt sienna, raw sienna, and burnt umber — will provide a nearly infinite range of realistic grime and rust colors for washes.

My technique with oils varies from acrylics. Start by putting small dabs of the oil colors into a paint tray or on a plain scrap piece of plastic and use a pipette to put some turpentine into a small bottle or into another recess in the paint tray.

Using a soft brush, either touch the tips of the bristles to the desired color or colors, then touch the bristle tips to the turpentine, or do the opposite; you'll get different effects with each. You can then brush the surface; the colors will flow with the turpentine. If doing a car side, start at the top, as the color will be strongest at the start of the brush stroke. Use as wide a brush as possible, and bring it down in a smooth motion following the vertical lines of the car.

This technique is very forgiving, as oils have a long drying time. If the first attempt isn't quite right (in color, or perhaps a wavy pattern), try it again. A brush with clean turpentine will take things off if you need to start over.

Once you get a good effect, leave it alone! Even when the turpentine evaporates and the surface looks dry, the oil paints will still be tacky. It will take a day or two for even thin paint washes to dry, several days if you have painted patches with full-strength paint.

Stains are like washes, but designed to penetrate porous material, namely wood. Commercial wood stain works well; you can also make stains from thinned paint. Cotton swabs make handy applicators; wipe any excess with a rag or paper towel.

STAINS

Stains are basically the same as washes, but they're applied to a porous surface that will absorb the color, such as wood. You can use a number of products and colors on wood (strip and sheet products or structure kit walls) depending upon the desired final effect.

Bare wood has a distinct look, ranging from a pale buff color with yellow, red, or green tinges depending upon the species of tree from which it came. Exposed wood in real life rarely maintains its color for long, however, as Mother Nature ages it to various shades of gray and brown.

Prototype lumber designed to remain outdoors is chemically treated with creosote or other products to preserve it. This includes railroad ties, utility poles, and wood on flatcar decks and loading platforms. Treated lumber often starts out nearly black or dark brown, and over the years lightens, turning dark or medium gray or brown.

One of the best ways to stain wood is with — you guessed it — wood stain! Commercial wood stains are available in a tremendous variety of colors, and standard small (eight-ounce) tins are relatively inexpensive. They're designed to be applied by brushing them on, letting them sit briefly to penetrate, then wiping off the excess. I usually apply them with a cotton swab (or a brush for larger surfaces), then use a paper towel to wipe the surface. (Use mineral spirits to clean brushes.)

Chapter 6 shows examples of staining wood with thinned acrylic paint in alcohol. I use black, dark gray, and dark or medium brown, starting with a mix of roughly 10% paint and 90% thinner. I try to follow photos or real-life examples in aiming for a specific color or effect.

With any of these materials and techniques, let the stains dry completely before gluing or working with the finished wood components, as expansion and contraction (and sometimes minor warping) can occur. And it's always a good idea to stain wood before gluing components together, as any stray glue at joints will keep stains from penetrating the wood.

DRYBRUSHING

Drybrushing is a simple technique where you get just a bit of paint on the bristles of a brush, wipe most of it off on a card or paper towel, then brush the model surface with the nearly dry brush. It works well for simulating streaked effects, such as a rust stain downward from a rust patch, grime and dirt stains that have tracked down the side of a car or locomotive, or streaked and peeling paint and lettering. It's also effective for highlighting raised details, such as rivet lines, weld seams, or complex detail parts.

It's usually most effective with a stiff-bristle brush; hog-bristle brushes also work well. Many modelers use old brushes for drybrushing, as the paint tends to dry on the bristles, which is hard on brushes.

How wet you want the paint to be depends on the effect you're trying to capture. You may find that using a fine-tip brush to actually paint the effect works best and gives you more control than drybrushing.

Drybrushing is also very effective when combined with other techniques. An example is painting a rust patch on a model, and when it dries, adding drybrushed streaks below it. You can then finish with a wash, overspray, or chalk effects to tie everything together.

With drybrushing, get paint on the bristle tips only, then wipe most of it off on a card or paper towel. Streak the resulting nearly dry brush on the surface. It's great for simulating rust streaks, peeling paint, and general grime. The hopper car then received a dusting of dark-gray chalk.

OVERSPRAYS

If you own an airbrush, it can be valuable for spraying thinned mixes (see the mixing advice for acrylic washes) on models. They're best for creating effects such as soot and exhaust stains, as well as dust, sand, dirt, grime, and stains from loads (such as coal or cement) — anything where a light shading with soft edges is desired.

Black to dark gray is best for exhaust effects, with dark grays and browns for general grime, tan and light brown for dust effects on trucks and the lower parts of rolling stock sides, and medium to dark brown and reddish-brown for rust effects.

Start with a mix of roughly 10% paint and 90% thinner. Use low pressure (around 15 psi) and keep the brush moving; the mix should appear wet when it hits the model surface, but should dry within a few seconds. If it stays wet too long or is applied too heavily, it can pool and create undesired patterns and stains. Practice on scrap materials until you get the effect you want. It often takes several coats to build up the effect. To protect the effects, add a clear flat finish when you're done.

POWDERED CHALKS

Chalks are a handy way to create many of the same effects as oversprays, where a feathered, dusty appearance is needed, such as exhaust, coal dust, grime, and rust. They can also be used in many cases to highlight raised details or create streaks and other effects (makeup, shown in Chapter 2, falls into the same category). It's absolutely vital with chalks to apply them to a dead-flat surface.

For soot and other dusty appearances, use black to dark gray (lighter grays can be effective on dark surfaces). Various browns work well for simulating rusted surfaces, with tans for sand and some soil and dirt effects. White and light gray work well for creating the effect of faded, bleached paint.

I like to put some chalk on a plain piece of card; it's easier to control this way, rather than sticking a brush directly into a container. You can also easily blend colors this way. For overall

CORRECTING A BAD WASH EFFECT

Sometimes weathering doesn't go as planned. This HO refrigerator car, a project of 20 years ago, received a black wash that proved to be way too heavy-handed to be realistic. My first mistake was using a wash that was too heavy (I should have added more thinner). My second mistake was not realizing that fact immediately after applying it. In addition to gathering around details, the mix swirled unrealistically on smooth surfaces between the rivet lines.

If this happens, quickly brushing water or alcohol across the areas will lessen and correct the effect. You can also blot up excess wash with a rag or paper towel, then apply more alcohol to rinse the wash away.

I didn't do that, instead hoping that the effect would fix itself as it dried. It didn't.

Once the wash was dry, fixing it became much more difficult. My first attempt was using common rubbing alcohol (70%) on a rag to wipe it away, which didn't work. I then brushed 91% isopropyl alcohol on the surface, left it for a minute, then rubbed it again. This worked to remove some of the wash effects from the smooth areas, but I had to be careful not to rub too much, as the underlying paint began to soften, as well.

My cleanup effort wasn't perfect, but it removed the worst of the undesired color and effects while leaving the grimy appearance around rivets and details, which is what I was aiming for. A bit of additional weathering, and the car will soon be ready for service.

The moral of the story: If something goes awry with paint, try to fix it quickly before it dries. And if it dries, try progressively stronger solutions to fix it.

An overdone wash effect applied 20 years earlier resulted in unrealistic blotching on this HO scale InterMountain refrigerator car. I pulled the model out of storage and saved it by scrubbing it with 91% rubbing alcohol, giving the car a much more realistically grimy appearance.

If you have an airbrush, you'll find it to be a valuable weathering tool. Here Cody Grivno is adding a spilled cement-dust effect to an HO covered hopper with thinned gray acrylic paint. Cody Grivno

dusty, feathered effects, use a soft-bristle brush and dip the bristles into the chalk. "Poof" the chalk onto the surface, vertically jabbing the brush downward and also using it to spread the chalk across all areas.

You'll reach a point where the chalk has covered as much as it's going to. Lightly blow off any excess, and be careful not to touch the areas you've done, as fingerprints will show (wearing rubber gloves is a good idea). Hit the chalk with a quick, light coat of clear flat to seal it. If needed, you can then add another coat of chalk or additional effects.

You can also use a stiff brush to apply chalk. This works well when you're trying to work chalk into crevices or tight areas (such as screens, fans, and louvers). You can use the brush to literally grind the chalk into place to create effects. You can also use a stiff brush to create streaks with chalk, such as below a grill and down the side of a diesel locomotive.

If a chalk effect isn't turning out as desired, a stiff brush will usually remove most of it. You can also rinse the model or use a damp cloth to remove the chalk and start over.

CHALK PASTE

If you want to create a rust patch with more texture than simply using paint, you can do this by making a paste of chalk and acrylic clear flat finish. Place a small pile of brown chalk on a scrap piece of card or plastic (I like to use the tip of a hobby knife blade as a shovel to get a small, precise amount). Place a drop or two of clear flat finish next to it, then use a small toothpick to mix some of the chalk into the clear flat until you have a blob of colored paste.

Apply it to the surface of the model using a toothpick or small brush. Once it dries, you'll have a very convincing rust patch that has a bit of three-dimensional texture to it. You can do this in layers with varying colors to build up effects. (See Chapter 10 on vehicles for an example.)

Powdered chalk can be applied with either a soft- or stiff-bristle (shown) brush, depending upon the desired effect. A dead-flat finish is imperative for providing "tooth" for getting the chalk to adhere to the surface. Here I'm adding the effect of dust kicked up by the wheels onto the lower areas of an F unit diesel.

PanPastels are a cake-style pigment that can be applied with a makeup sponge (shown) or brush. They work well for a variety of rust and grime effects.

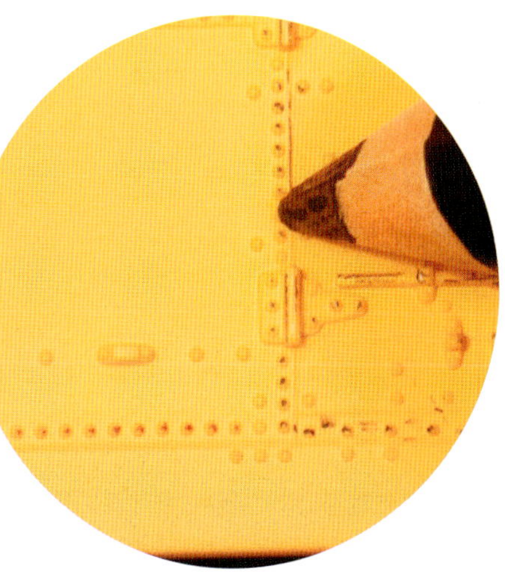

Artist's pencils in various colors work for highlighting small, fine details such as the rivets and door details on this HO refrigerator car.

PANPASTELS

PanPastels are in a category by themselves. They are paint pigments, but are chalk-like in cake form. They are best applied with soft brushes or sponges (makeup sponges work very well). It's more difficult to create feathered effects with them compared to powdered chalks, but they're easier to control and great for creating many of the same effects as washes (but with more control).

Load the sponge by tapping it lightly onto the PanPastel, then softly brush it or dab it onto the surface. For a lighter effect, treat it like drybrushing and rub the brush or sponge onto a card first to remove some of the pigment.

PENCILS

Artist's pencils work well when you need precise control over an effect or color, such as highlighting rivet lines, raised details, or specific areas. Artist's chalk sticks and pastel crayons can be used in similar manner, but will have slightly broader tips and coverage areas.

Turn the page and we'll start putting techniques together to capture specific prototype effects.

CHAPTER FOUR

Freight car basic weathering

Freight cars are a perfect place to start experimenting with weathering techniques. Every layout has them (a lot of them, in many cases), and there's a wide variation in appearance among car types, eras, and old and new cars.

Left: This Bangor & Aroostook ice-bunker reefer was built in 1947 but repainted in the early 1960s; it's shown in 1968. It's in good shape but showing its age through a general coat of grime. Jeff Wilson collection

Below: This InterMountain HO model of a Spokane, Portland & Seattle boxcar has been weathered with a combination of oil-color washes, acrylic drybrushing, decal chalk marks, PanPastels, and detail painting. It also has a paper tag on its tackboard to alert yard crews to not sort it in a hump yard.

The wheels on this old solid-bearing truck are caked with grease and grime, showing texture. The sideframe shows a wide variety of color.

The roller-bearing trucks on this modern tank car are just a couple of years old. Note the rust-colored wheel faces, dark red roller-bearing adapters, and blue roller-bearing end caps. The sideframes are painted black. Cody Grivno

Paint the wheel faces a dark color (grimy black or rust) to kill the metallic shine (as on this metal wheelset) or eliminate the shiny black finish on engineering-plastic versions.

You can use many techniques to weather cars, but understanding how prototype cars weather and age will help you decide what methods to use and to what extent to carry the effects on your models. As with other models, the best way to achieve realistic results is to carefully look at prototype cars from the era being modeled and try to figure out the best way to duplicate them.

We'll start with a look at how prototype cars acquire their weathered appearance, including the effects of Mother Nature, heavy use, and vandalism. We'll then look at common components including wheels, trucks, couplers, and roofs. We'll then move to several projects showing individual cars of several types.

PROTOTYPE CARS

Prototype freight cars display a tremendous range in appearance based on their age. Freight cars can remain in service for a long time (currently a legal limit of 40 years, or 50 with rebuilding). However, they are rarely if ever washed. A steel car can go its entire service life with an occasional rain shower or thunderstorm being the only cleaning it will see.

Cars are sometimes repainted, but this generally only happens if they are rebuilt or undergo extensive repairs (wood-sheathed cars required more frequent repairs, and thus repainting). Many older cars that are sold to new owners are simply restenciled with new reporting marks and numbers. Some railroads were more finicky about repainting cars acquired by merger or sale; again, look to specific prototypes for examples.

In general, a car that's just a year or two old will typically look pretty new, with perhaps some dust and grime on the trucks. After a few years, paint often starts to fade; dings begin appearing, with dents, rust spots, and scrapes. Modern cars will often acquire various levels of graffiti.

By the time a car approaches 15 to 20 years old, it can really begin showing its age. Paint can be quite bleached, and lettering can peel and fade. Data has often been restenciled, and perhaps the car number and reporting marks have been changed, as well. Patches and repairs are sometimes visible as freshly painted areas.

Cars that make it to age 30 or older without being repainted will often look pretty beat up. Original lettering can be quite hard to see; large areas of rust or peeling paint may appear. Cars that have been sold to new owners will have new reporting marks, with old lettering and logos sometimes patched out. Graffiti may cover large portions of the sides.

How you apply this to freight cars on your layout depends largely upon the year or period you model. If you model 1972, then any cars built from the mid-1960s to 1972 should look pretty good, while cars built in the 1950s are showing heavier weathering effects. There should be fewer cars from the 1940s and earlier, and those still around should show the heaviest weathering effects unless they've been repainted. (For example, a Great Northern boxcar built in 1946 but repainted by Burlington Northern in 1971 would look like new.)

Let's look at some details and weathering effects that apply across all types of cars.

WHEELS AND TRUCKS

Wheels and trucks are subject to heavy weathering, as the wheels kick up grime and dirt on all components and the moving parts are subject to wear. Specific weathering patterns on trucks, however, largely depend on their type — specifically, whether they have solid-bearing or roller-bearing journals.

Into the 1960s, most trucks had solid-bearing journals (often incorrectly called "friction bearings"). These relied on journal boxes filled with grease or oil to lubricate the axle ends, which were carried by bearings within the boxes. These boxes had flip-up lids enabling workers to add more lubricant, which had to be done on a regular basis.

The effect of this was that grease leaking out of the boxes would often wind up on the wheel faces; this in turn attracted layers of dirt and grime. The resulting appearance was often

For added detail with solid-bearing trucks, press powdered chalk into the still-wet paint to provide texture.

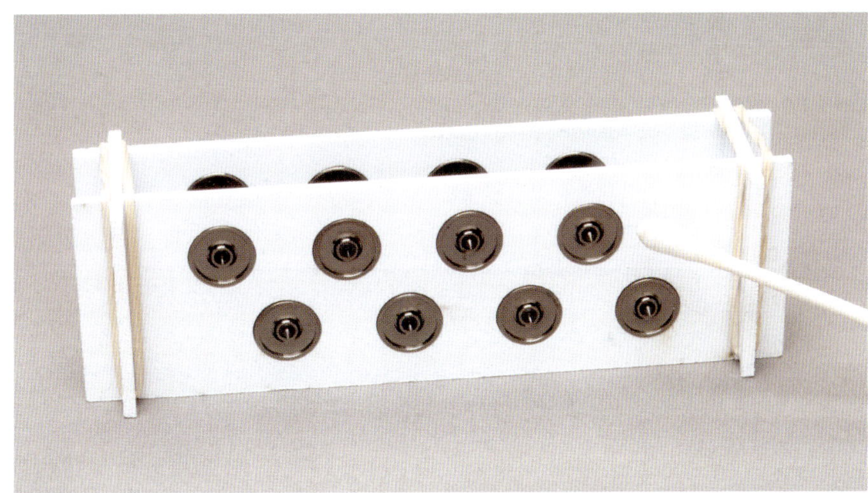

Jigs (such as this one from Modeler's Choice) make it easier to paint multiple wheels at once. If airbrushing, be sure to mask the needle points on the axles.

Pencils or wood dowels turned to a point, mounted to a base, make handy holders for airbrushing or brush-painting truck frames. Cody Grivno

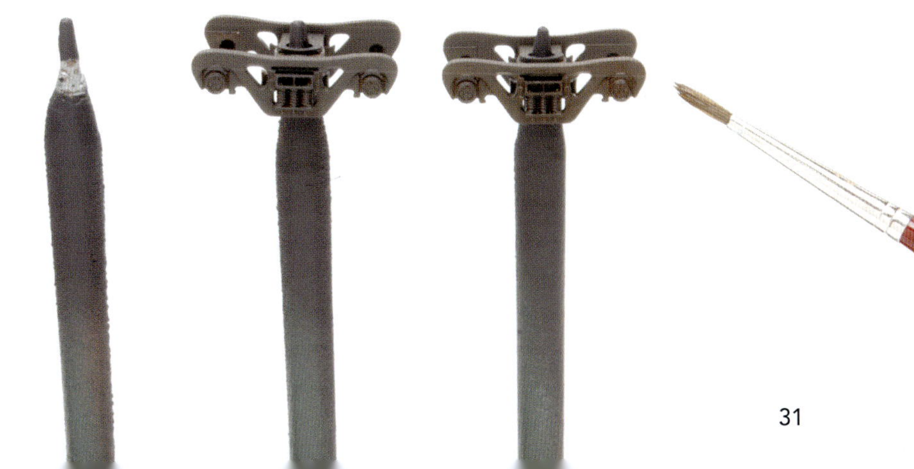

dark (near black) and oily, with a distinct texture. In addition, the journals and journal-box lids were often stained with oil.

The move to roller-bearing trucks began rapidly in the 1960s. On these trucks, the axle ends are supported by multiple cylindrical steel rollers (the roller bearings), held in a sealed unit that rarely requires maintenance or lubrication. The result is that the wheels don't acquire the grease/grime coating of those on solid-bearing trucks.

Since wheels aren't painted, wheel faces on roller-bearing trucks are typically a shade of rust, ranging from orange-light brown (on new trucks) and getting darker as they age, to shades of medium to dark brown — all with a flat finish.

The color of truck sideframes varies by railroad. The majority were painted black, but some were painted to match the car color (usually a shade of boxcar red or brown). All tend to weather to dark gray and rust colors; after 10 or 15 years, it can be difficult to determine their original color.

SOLID-BEARING TRUCKS AND WHEELS

ROLLER-BEARING TRUCKS AND WHEELS

Basic painting and weathering greatly improve the appearance of both solid-bearing (top) and roller-bearing (bottom) trucks and wheels.

The unpainted galvanized roof on this 20-year-old Detroit, Toledo & Ironton 86-foot boxcar has begun to weather and wear, with rusted areas on many panels. Note that other than the rust, the roof is rather clean. J. David Ingles

On roller-bearing trucks, the roller-bearing adapters (the brackets directly above the roller bearing caps) are often a shade of dark red or brown. On many modern trucks, the roller-bearing end caps are blue. Check prototype photos for the era you're modeling.

Roofs with worn paint can be simulated by painting silver to simulate where paint has worn and peeled to reveal the galvanized surface. Rust patches can then be added.

WEATHERING TRUCKS

For wheels, I usually start with a shade of rust-color acrylic paint on the wheel faces, applied with a brush. Be sure to paint the axles and rear of the wheels as well; these areas are more noticeable on some car types (tank cars, hoppers) than others.

On the faces of wheels on solid-bearing trucks, you can add a shade of grimy black or black, plus a coat of Polly Scale oily black. If you really want to take it to the next level, add texture by pressing some dark gray powdered chalk into the still-wet paint. The effect is pretty good, but you have to get close to see it.

For the truck sideframes, I usually put a few drops of black and various shades of brown on a card and brush paint the trucks with a mix of the colors. New trucks should be fairly uniform black or dark gray, with more brown and gray shading the older the car. A pencil or a dowel with the end turned to a point in a pencil sharpener will work well to hold the truck for painting (see page 31).

Paint the roller-bearing adapters and end caps with a fine-point brush if appropriate to the model. You can also add dark gray to the brake shoes.

Painting wheels and trucks is pretty straightforward when you only have one or two cars to do. Jigs can make painting multiple components easier and faster. The photo on page 31 shows a wheel holder from Modeler's Choice (No. 236), which is no longer made, but American Model Builders and MinuteMan Scale Models have offered similar jigs laser-cut from acrylic for several brands and wheel sizes.

If you're airbrushing wheel faces using jigs, be careful not to get paint on the needle-bearing axle ends.

How much care should you take in painting trucks? That depends on your modeling time and number of cars you

The top two HO boxcar roofs represent cars with worn, peeling paint, exposing bare silver-gray metal and patches of rust. The bottom roof represents an unpainted, rusting galvanized roof that also has yellow overspray from painting the car sides.

This laser-cut wood running board from American Model Builders is an easy-to-add replacement for the molded plastic versions of most HO boxcars. I stained it with a grimy black wash, then streaked boxcar red paint over it to simulate a worn — but structurally sound — assembly.

have to do. Even though these details are largely hidden in shadows under cars, a lack of weathering that reveals shiny plastic is usually apparent.

If you have a large layout with lots of cars, a cursory coat of paint will likely suffice. If you have a small switching layout with few cars, where operators are close to the action, give the wheels and trucks more attention.

CAR ROOFS

Roofs on "house cars" (boxcars, stockcars, refrigerator cars) are largely above our line of sight and therefore out of mind when we're out railfanning. However, on our models, they're quite prominent, since we're often looking down on our modeled scenes.

Before you begin weathering roofs, I highly recommend going to a bridge or other elevated viewing area where you can look down on passing trains. What you see might change both your thinking on how cars weather and how you approach your modeling.

Roofs do indeed take a beating, but not in the way many modelers think. Since the 1930s, most roofs have been made from galvanized (coated with zinc) stamped steel panels that are either left unpainted, painted the car color, or coated with black roofing cement over the galvanized coating.

Over time on painted roofs, the paint over the galvanized coating wears off, revealing the coating (which then gradually rusts in patches); on unpainted roofs, the coating weathers over time and areas often rust, especially if they've been dinged or scraped.

So what's the revelation? Freight car roofs are usually much cleaner than we realize. The sun's rays bleach the paint, and although driving rain leads to rust, it also washes most grime off the roof and down the car sides. The result is a dead-flat finish, bleached, with some cars showing rust patches that range from small areas to near-total coverage.

My recommendation is to go lightly on grime and soot effects (although the nature of steam locomotives meant almost everything was sootier into the 1950s). Vary the appearance among cars, following the earlier guidelines about the relative ages of cars helping dictate the level of weathering effects.

BASIC ROOF EFFECTS

Most factory-painted cars simply use silver paint to represent galvanized roofs, but this is too bright to accurately represent galvanized metal. The photos in Chapter 1 show a basic starting point for roofs with a simple coat of clear flat acrylic and possibly a light grimy black wash. If you're painting a model, mix silver about 50:50 with light gray for a better effect.

Modeling the effects of a painted roof with paint peeling from the galvanized coating is easy with a brush and flat silver paint or silver/gray mix, as the photos on page 33 show. I used Polly Scale flat silver in various patterns. You can add rust effects with various brown colors.

Another effect you'll find, especially on cars since the 1960s, is overspray from painting the car sides. No attempt is made to mask the roof when cars are painted, so galvanized roofs on these cars often show a light shadow of the car color around the edges.

This can be eye-catching on a model. The best way to simulate it is by airbrushing a thinned mix of the car color, just as on the prototype. If you don't have an airbrush, you can use powdered chalk of the right color.

WEATHERED ROOF CEMENT

Charlie Duckworth modeled the roof on this Tichy HO boxcar to represent an older boxcar with a roof coated in cement that has begun to wear and flake away. Charlie mixed black and white oil paints and applied various hues of dark gray patches near the running board and some of the ribs. He then mixed a light gray color and outlined the patches with a small brush.

The dark paint represents the car cement, while the light around the edges denotes recently exposed galvanized metal that hasn't weathered yet.

After allowing the oil paint to dry for an hour, he lightly drybrushed over the two colors to soften the edges and give the roof a faded look.

Roof cement was common on wood cars and many early steel cars. It tended to wear away over time. Charlie Duckworth

When you're done, brush or spray a coat of clear flat on the roof, and if you choose, a light coat of a grimy weathering spray or chalk dusting to tone down the silver and blend all of the effects.

From the steam to early diesel eras there were other types of roofs, as well. Some early refrigerator cars had wood roofs covered by tarpaper and roofing tar; other roofs were wood with tin panels on top. These could be painted and/or coated with roof cement.

Walkways atop house cars ("running boards" is the correct term, not "roof walks") were standard equipment until the mid-1960s, when they were banned. They were then gradually removed from older cars. Running boards were wood (three side-by-side planks) through the 1940s, when steel (grating-style) running boards began appearing.

Wood running boards usually start out painted the car color, but after a few years the paint usually wore away to reveal weathered wood. You can simulate this by streaking factory-painted plastic running boards with various shades of gray to simulate paint wearing away.

You can also swap the plastic part for actual wood planks or laser-cut versions (American Model Builders and others have made them). I treat these by staining the wood various shades of gray, then drybrushing and applying washes of the body color. An interesting detail can be a freshly painted plank to signify a recent repair was made to an older car.

Some steel running boards were left unpainted (galvanized), but others were painted the car color. The molded versions on most kits are quite thick compared to the real thing; if the depressions simulating the open grating are deep enough, a black wash can be effective in creating a look of depth. You can also replace them with aftermarket parts, such as etched-metal details from Detail Associates, Overland Models, or Plano, or plastic ones from Kadee.

An important factor to remember about running boards and other safety devices: You can model them as being quite weathered, but never broken. A broken or missing plank on a running board would cause the car to be immediately bad-ordered to the shop for repairs.

COUPLERS, HOSES, AND TACK BOARDS

Painting and weathering details — whether they are separate parts or molded in place — can greatly improve freight car appearance.

UNDERFRAMES

Underframes are often afterthoughts on freight car models. Prototype underframes and underbody components (brake gear and rods) often start out painted black or oxide red, but soon fade to grimy black with rust.

On many models, underframes are largely hidden, as on most boxcars, other house cars, and most gondolas and flatcars. However, many components can indeed be seen when models are viewed at eye level, and the shiny black plastic in which they're often molded can be a distraction.

The best solution is to give everything under the car a coat of flat grimy black or dark brown paint. This doesn't have to be done neatly, and complete coverage isn't even needed — just enough to kill the shine on anything visible and present a mottled, grimy appearance.

I generally use a medium-sized flat brush and slap a coat of paint on as best as I can, making sure I get the sides of the center sill (especially behind the trucks), the sides of the coupler box, and any rods and brake gear hanging from the frame.

On other types of cars, the undergear and frame are more visible (many covered hoppers, tank cars, and open hoppers). With those, treat these areas with the same care as you would with a car side.

Air hoses receive a coat of grimy black paint, with light gray on the glad hand and upper pipe/angle cock. The coupler received a mix of grimy black and dark brown.

Prototype couplers are unpainted and range in color from light rust to dark brown. They can be painted by brush with a palette of rust-colored acrylics, but the paint will likely flake off the front of the knuckles as they are used. This is fine, as it gives them a varied appearance. If you keep the metal uncoupling pins, paint them flat black; you generally want these unprototypical items to disappear from view as much as possible.

Many ready-to-run cars today include air hoses. These range from pretty good to unrealistically small and poorly located. My general preference is remove them if they don't look good and replace them with aftermarket hoses (my favorite for HO is Cal-Scale), especially for cars with their uncoupling pins removed. Paint these grimy black, with a touch of medium to dark gray at the ends (the metal glad hand) and at their mounting location to simulate the metal valve handle (angle cock).

Steel house cars have a large and small tack board on the sides and ends. The specific locations vary; many are on doors. These are wood panels that give agents and shippers a place to staple notes about loads, handling and unloading instructions, and routing and train information (on the small route board). Wood cars didn't have these, as notes could be tacked directly to the car sides.

These are painted the car color, but as they are used and age, the paint can peel, showing gray streaks where the weathered wood shows through. You can simulate this by streaking them with a brush. Several companies offer notes that can be glued to the boards (the boxcar on page 28 shows a Do Not Hump note). A small piece of plain paper can suffice, since lettering would be tough to read in smaller scales.

Molded-on details can be highlighted with artist's pencils, washes, or drybrushing. This includes door latches, door hinges (on refrigerator cars), rivet lines, and weld seams. These tend to accumulate dirt and grime, and they show shadows in real life that can be tough to see on modeled versions.

It might not technically be "weathering," but depending upon the era you model, look for small decal details to add, including consolidated stencils (starting in the late 1960s), ACI panels (late 1960s-late 1970s), and wheel-inspection dots (late 1970s).

CHALK MARKS

Through the 1960s, agents often labeled cars with chalk marks to indicate train routing, train number, destination, or other special instructions. This is not graffiti; it's to aid fellow railroaders. This is why cabooses, yard offices, and depots had fat sticks of chalk in a rack near the doorway.

Being chalk, these markings tended to fade rather quickly, but depending upon their service, some cars acquired quite a collection of markings. These would be a mix, with some bright and new and others faded.

Microscale, Clover House (dry transfers), Protocraft, and National Scale Car have all offered decal sets for these, and discontinued sets by Sunshine Models sometimes turn up at dealers or on eBay. The boxcar on page 38 shows several of these; other cars throughout this book also bear them.

Applying them is easy: paint a small area with clear gloss to provide a smooth surface for application, then add them as with any other decal. To get the effect of mixed fresh and faded marks, apply them in layers. Add one or two of them, then a coat of chalk or wash of the car color, then another one or two marks. Keep repeating until you have the effect you're looking for.

You can also make your own with white or light gray artist's pencil. Use a light touch and make sure the pencil has a sharp point.

Tack boards are located on the ends and sides of most steel house cars. They're originally painted the car color, but as this boxcar shows, the paint eventually wears away, revealing weathered wood.

Through the 1960s, chalk marks were commonly used by yard agents and clerks to indicate routing, train numbers, interchange, and other information. Decal sets for these have been made by several companies; the car on page 28 has markings from Sunshine Models sets. John Ingles

GRAFFITI

Few things regarding painting and weathering stir such strong feelings among modelers as graffiti. It's certainly become a prevalent feature on freight cars in the past couple of decades, but some modelers hate modeling it, believing that doing so is essentially glorifying vandalism. Other modelers see graffiti as a common feature that must be included in order to capture realism.

I'm not going to tell you which camp to join, but if you decide to add graffiti to freight cars, there are a couple ways to go about it. You can keep it simple and/or humorous if you choose, or you can apply extensive graffiti to match prototype examples.

You'll find several varieties of graffiti on prototype cars, greatly ranging in complexity, almost always applied via spray cans. The simplest is basic tagging, with text scrawled on: this includes names, slogans, profanity, or gang affiliations. At the other extreme are complex designs of multi colors that can take up an entire car side.

The easiest way to model graffiti is with commercial decals offered by Microscale and others. Adding these is as simple as applying any other decal to a car. For older cars, you can apply various weathering effects first, then add the decals to indicate recently added graffiti.

Another way of creating graffiti is with paint markers or gel pens, which are available in a variety of colors. Your artistic talents will dictate the extent that you can do this realistically.

When placing graffiti, remember that the lowest points on the car side are the places most commonly hit.

As with other weathering, keep it varied. Older graffiti is often covered by grime or rust, or even by newer graffiti. Graffiti that covers the reporting marks and number is usually painted out quickly with a patch and new numbers and letters, which may be stenciled or painted in freehand style.

Decals are available for various types of graffiti; this is Microscale set No. 87-1139.

Paint markers work well for creating graffiti. For a *Model Railroader* article, M.R. Snell demonstrated how he used blue for the main lettering, then outlined it in white. Two photos: M.R. Snell

CHAPTER FIVE

Boxcar and reefer projects

Now that we've looked at techniques and specific freight car details, let's dive in with a couple of projects involving house cars — enclosed freight cars. Don't necessarily look at these as specific projects to follow; instead, let them provide inspiration for prototype cars you'd like to duplicate, following the idea of adding various weathering effects in layers.

This former Railbox car was built in the mid-1970s, acquired by Burlington Northern in 1984, and photographed in 1994. It bears fading paint and lettering, has many rust patches, has acquired a layer of grime, and has been restenciled and renumbered for its new owner.

This HO scale 50-foot boxcar represents a former Railbox car acquired by Burlington Northern. Weathering is a mix of acrylic paints, thinned oversprays, and washes, applied in layers.

FORMER RAILBOX CAR

An example of an older freight car that has been sold to a secondary owner is this former Railbox (RBOX) car that was built in the 1970s and in the next decade sold to Burlington Northern and restenciled. The weathering, faded lettering, and restenciling made it a challenging — but very doable — project.

Railbox boxcars began appearing in the mid-1970s. Owned by a group of railroads and managed as a subsidiary of Trailer Train, Railbox cars were "pool" cars, meaning they could be reloaded for any destination on any railroad, and didn't have to follow standard car use rules that routed cars back to their home railroads.

The prototype photo is from 1994, when the car was approaching 20 years old, and 11 years after BN had acquired and restenciled it. The key elements to capture were the faded areas of original lettering, the overall cast of grime, several rust patches and streaks, and the bright yellow areas and

The prototype roof (top) is weathered but fairly clean, and it shows the yellow overspray from when the sides were painted. The model (bottom) had a silver roof. I airbrushed thinned yellow around the edges to match typical prototype cars. I also added some rust patches and gave the roof an overspray of thinned black.

newer lettering of the restenciling.

The model is a stock HO scale Accurail 50-foot exterior-post boxcar lettered for Railbox. It's not completely accurate for this prototype, but was close enough for my goal of capturing the overall appearance of the restenciled car.

My first step was the roof, which I did following the steps shown in Chapter 4. I gave the factory-painted silver roof an airbrushed coat of thinned black to dull it and make it look more like galvanized metal. I then gave the edges a light airbrushed coat of thinned yellow to simulate the overspray often found on these cars (as seen in the prototype photo). I followed with some brushed rust colors on a few panels. The finished roof can be seen in Chapter 4 (page 33).

On the sides, I first tried to remove some of the logo on the right side, but none of the usual solutions worked, and 91% alcohol began removing the body paint as well. Instead, I decided to use yellow acrylic paint, dabbed on with a makeup sponge. The yellow doesn't cover well, so it took a few coats. I followed this with a coat of clear acrylic flat, airbrushed on.

NICKEL PLATE BOXCAR

This Nickel Plate boxcar illustrates what a few relatively simple coats of weathering will do to an otherwise stock, simple kit — in this case an HO Accurail 40-foot car lettered for NKP. The sides were given a wash of thinned acrylic black, followed by a mix of black and brown powdered chalk and PanPastels to re-create the areas of dark and light weathering on the side of the prototype car. The trucks and roof were treated as shown in Chapter 4. Everything was sealed with a coat of clear flat finish.

My goal was to capture the overall effects of the prototype car shown below. The key is figuring out the colors needed, then choosing the materials to best represent them.

This paint on this 1948-built Nickel Plate Road 40-foot boxcar has largely turned to rusted areas by this late 1960s image. Note the oily appearance of the wheel faces, caused by oil seeping from journal boxes.
J. David Ingles

I applied PanPastels with a makeup sponge to highlight areas of the original car color, as well as for grimy areas.

I faded the logo and some of the weathering by using a makeup sponge to dab yellow paint over the areas (top and left). It took a few coats to get the effect I was looking for, as yellow doesn't cover well.

One method of simulating faded or bleached paint is by rubbing white chalk into the surface (bottom). Make sure the surface has a dead-flat finish before applying chalk.

50-FOOT BOXCAR

Robert Putnam did a fine job of detail weathering this Athearn 50-foot boxcar to represent a car built in the late 1970s that had been in service for a decade. It was typical of the colorful IPD ("incentive-per-diem") boxcars owned by shortlines and leased by the thousands beginning in the late 1970s.

Robert faded the model's factory paint job with a light airbrush coat of thinned white paint. The bulk of the weathering is rust-color oil paints, applied with a fine-tip brush. Capturing the dozens of simulated dings and scratches in the paint was time-consuming, but results in an extremely realistic appearance. He also painted large rust areas on the door, door tracks, and streaks downward from the exterior posts.

After allowing the oil paints to dry completely, Robert finished the weathering with brown and black weathering powders on the sides, roof, and ends. The car is a great example of what can be accomplished by taking your time while using simple techniques.

Incentive-per-diem (IPD) boxcars were built by the thousands in bright paint schemes for dozens of short lines in the late 1970s. Robert Putnam's HO Athearn model nicely captures the typical look of these cars as they aged in the 1990s and later. Robert Putnam

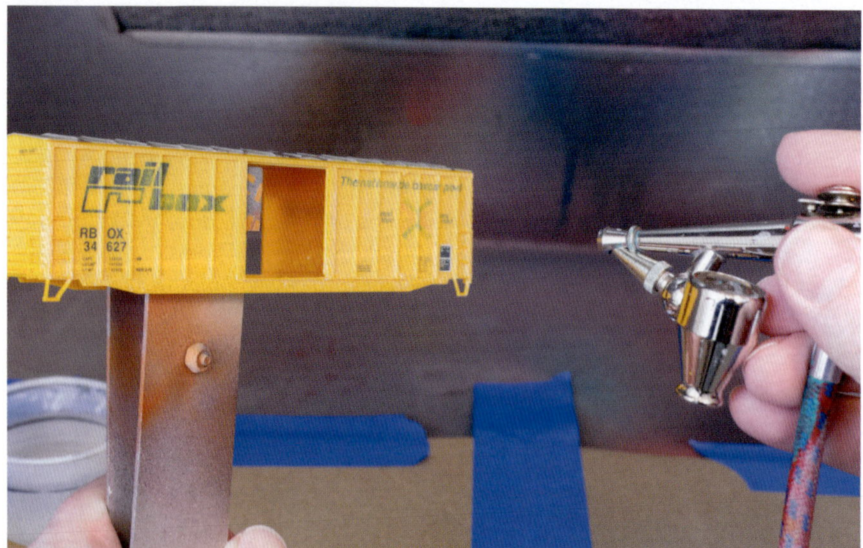

Another way to fade paint is by using an airbrush to apply thinned white paint (about 15% paint to 85% thinner). Go slowly and work in layers; trying to do too much too quickly will result in runs and blobs.

A wash of thinned black acrylic paint provided a grimy, streaked appearance and highlighted the vertical posts.

The rusted areas were brush-painted with various shades of brown acrylic paint, then streaked with a wider brush before they dried.

Fading the paint (and further fading the lettering) can be done a couple of ways. After giving the sides a coat of clear flat, I started on one side with an application of white powdered chalk, really working it into the surface. This toned down the yellow, making it look slightly bleached from age. On the other side I tried a light overspray of thinned white acrylic, applying it over the faded lettering.

The patchout was simple. I just brush-painted over the factory-applied reporting marks and number with yellow paint (it took a couple of coats). The new numbers and letters are from a Microscale alphabet/number set — the exact size and style weren't critical. I also painted out the capacity data with light gray paint to match the prototype car, then applied new numbers scavenged from an old decal set. When they dried, I brush-painted clear flat acrylic over those panels.

I followed this by brushing a wash of thinned black (acrylic paint in its own thinner) down the sides and external posts. This added overall grime as well as streaks. I did this after the restenciling, since the car had, in theory, run for 10 years since its relettering.

Next came individual rust patches, which on the prototype car looked like the aftermath of some dings and scratches. I brush-painted the patches with a couple shades of dark brown acrylic paint, then when they were almost dry, streaked them downward with a wide brush. A light coat of clear flat finish sealed all of the weathering and completed the model.

FORMER GM&O BOXCAR

The idea for this heavily weathered model of a former Gulf, Mobile & Ohio boxcar came from a Dave Ingles slide taken in 1996. The prototype photo shows a car built around 1960 that at some point — likely in the late 1980s — was sold to regional railroad Chicago, Central & Pacific.

My starting point for this one is an Accurail HO model factory painted in green for GM&O. My goal wasn't striving for an exact match to the prototype car, but creating a car that

This Accurail HO boxcar started out in Gulf, Mobile & Ohio's green scheme. It's been weathered to represent a car that's been in service 30-plus years and sold to a regional railroad.

captured the flavor and overall effects. I weathered this car in two stages — stopping at the midpoint would have yielded a nicely weathered car representing its likely appearance in the mid-1970s. After pausing, I continued adding effects to bring it to a mid-1990s look.

I had assembled the car for an earlier project. A few years ago, it took a dive off my workbench and broke a side door, but surprisingly had no other damage. I took the opportunity to do what the prototype often does in those situations and scavenged a replacement door from a long-forgotten kit in my scrapbox. The door was boxcar red and I left it that way, as the real railroad would likely have done when making a quick repair on an older car like this.

After giving the car a coat of clear flat finish, I painted some rust-colored streaks down the car sides and over the lettering. I drybrushed some horizontal rust streaks to the right of the door to simulate scratches from opening and closing. A piece of thin card with a slot cut in it with a hobby knife provided a guide to keep these streaks straight and horizontal.

I added decals for the consolidated stencils, ACI label, and wheel-inspection dot to the right end of the side and some chalk marks on the far

This boxcar was built for GM&O around 1960. Successor Illinois Central Gulf sold it to Chicago, Central & Pacific in the early 1990s. J. David Ingles

A simple cardboard stencil works well when you need to keep weathering effects (in this case drybrushing to simulate scrapes from the door sliding) in alignment. They also work well for rivet lines and weld seams.

The first layer of weathering includes simulated horizontal scrapes and rust caused by the door, plus oil-paint rust streaks down the sides and over the lettering. The ACI label, wheel-inspection dot, and consolidated stencil boxes are all from Microscale.

After further weathering on the sides, I added another chalk-mark decal, painted out the capacity data, and added new capacity decals from a scrap decal set. Here I'm adding decal-setting solution.

At this point you could call it completed and have a nice car for a late 1970s/early 1980s layout. I used a cotton swab dipped in water to remove a bit of weathering from the consolidated stencils, replicating what a prototype car agent may have done when updating data on it.

To bring the model into the 1990s, I painted out the road name with grimy black using a brush (I later touched this up with darker gray when the original paint didn't stand out enough), then added additional weathering to the sides to better represent the prototype car.

left side. I painted the areas with clear gloss before adding the decals. When these dried, I brushed over them with clear flat.

The entire car received a wash of thinned black acrylic. The roof was given some rust and weathered silver patches to simulate a galvanized roof that had been painted and is now peeling (see Chapter 4).

The capacity data and reweigh date are restenciled. I did this by brush-painting boxcar red over the old data, then adding new numbers left over from an old set of freight-car decals. I also added another chalk-mark decal, which will wind up being cleaner than the previously applied marks.

The car as it stood at that point would be ready for service on a late-1970s layout. I contemplated stopping at this point, but decided to keep going to more closely represent the prototype car.

I used grimy black to brush-paint over the arched road name lettering on the left side, then the old reporting marks (but not the number). I also painted over the old "RETURN TO …" stenciling near the door. An interesting thing on the prototype was that the CC&P kept the car's original number, but added a "1" in front of it, so I did the same on the model (with similar lack of care for the size and spacing of the new numeral).

Finishing the car was a matter of applying additional grime weathering, which I did with an extra wash, followed by dark gray PanPastels applied with a sponge. The trucks were done as described in Chapter 4. A light coat of clear flat finish completed this boxcar project.

WILSON WOOD REFRIGERATOR CAR

Ice-bunker refrigerator cars are an example of freight cars that weather in a particular way. The inspiration for this project was a wood-sheathed car owned by Union Refrigerator Transit and leased to the Soo Line. A pronounced feature on this car, found relatively often on wood-sheathed cars, was a series of boards that had been repaired and either cleaned or

Repaired side boards were a common feature on wood-sheathed refrigerator cars. Other weathering on this HO Red Caboose model includes oil-paint washes, drybrushed streaks showing effects of salt/brine by the roof hatches, and powdered-chalk grime.

This prototype Union Refrigerator wood-sheathed reefer (leased to Soo Line) was built in 1921 and rebuilt in 1955. It's showing a layer of grime by this 1962 photo, but with repaired boards on the side and door. The seams between the vertical tongue-in-groove boards are readily visible. J. David Ingles

The roof received a wash of thinned black paint plus some rusted areas. The simulated wood boards on the hatches and running board received gray dry-brushing to simulate paint wearing away.

Masking the "repaired" boards before weathering will keep them clean. Here I'm following an oil-paint wash with some powdered chalk to simulate accumulated grime.

repainted, while the rest of the car remained grimy. The car also provided a chance to add weathering showing wear on the roof and residue from the salt and ice mixture used to chill ice-bunker cars, especially ones in meat service.

I started with a ready-to-run Red Caboose HO model of a 36-foot Mather refrigerator car, factory-painted for Wilson & Co. This was a car in dedicated meat service for its owner.

Simulating the repaired boards was easy. I applied thin strips of masking tape to cover several vertical boards just to the left of the door on one side before beginning weathering.

The door hinges were painted with a rust-colored wash, as shown in Chapter 3. The sides then received a light wash of brown oil paints thinned with turpentine, which both provided a grimy cast to the car and also highlighted the simulated separations between the tongue-and-groove vertical boards.

I also added rust patches and dark streaks on the frame and side sill below the side boards. The trucks and underframe received various rust and dark gray colors as with other cars.

On the roof, I gave all the roof panels a wash of brown and black oil

Bob Rivard used oil paints and turpentine to create this weathered former Duluth, South Shore & Atlantic boxcar for his HO Soo Line layout. Two photos: Bob Rivard

DOUBLE-DOOR DSS&A BOXCAR

Bob Rivard captured the look of an older boxcar that has been restenciled for a new owner. He painted this HO InterMountain 50-foot double-door boxcar and lettered it for Duluth, South Shore & Antlantic with Microscale decals (set MC-4112).

Bob then used oil paints in rust and grime colors and turpentine to create the many rust patches and the large scraped area to the right of the doors. He created the patch-out effect at left and added Soo Line lettering to represent a car after the DSS&A merged into Soo Line. Bob then further postdated the car by adding an ACI label (the colored barcode at right) and chalk mark decals, followed with an overspray of thinned black.

Bob created the rust patches with oil paints, then streaked them downward before they completely dried.

paints, and also added some simulated rust patches and stains. The ice hatches, which are simulated wood, received dark gray drybrushing to simulate peeling and worn paint. The running board received similar treatment. I let the oil paints dry thoroughly, then added some powdered black chalk to the sides and ends for an additional grimy effect.

These cars often had salt added to their ice loads in the bunkers (used to cool the cars further by accelerating the rate of melting). The salt and resulting brine often stained the roof and sides near the hatches. I captured this by drybrushing light gray streaks on these areas, extending down the sides.

The salt also caused rust to form quickly on many cars. I added rust patches with both oils and acrylics to the edge of the roof, on some door components, on the ladder, and on the side sill, and streaked the colors down the sides with a brush to simulate staining (since the wood itself won't rust).

Peeling off the masking tape revealed the "repaired" boards, and a coat of clear flat finished the car.

CHAPTER SIX

Gondolas, flatcars, and hoppers

Open cars (gondolas, flats, and hoppers) offer unique opportunities for weathering, with their open decks and interior surfaces. Even relatively new cars will show heavy signs of use in a short time. Modeling this wear will lead to more realistic models.

Gondolas are among the most beat-up freight cars on railroads. This Life-Like HO model of a mill gondola has been weathered with real rust on the floor, plus oil paint washes on the sides and interior walls.

I placed several pieces of rusted metal in a small container, then crushed them into smaller pieces with the plastic end of a tool handle. The results can be sifted and sorted for various uses.

Paint the floor with a heavy coat of dark brown acrylic paint, then pour the rust onto the wet paint. Use a brush to distribute the rust pieces to uncovered areas. The paint will secure the rust in place.

GONDOLA WITH REAL RUST

Gondolas are probably the most beat-up cars on the railroad. They are the pickup trucks of railroading, carrying everything from scrap metal to steel components to — especially in the steam era — aggregates and coal.

As a result, gons get pretty dinged up in service. This shows as dents, scrapes, and resulting rust and rust streaks, especially on the floor and interior walls, as well as on the sides and across the lettering. Interior scrapes and rust are prominent, with debris from various loads.

On this car, I wanted to try using real rust as the weathering agent. Real rust has a texture and color variation that is tough to capture with paint, so the real thing can be a valuable material to have on hand.

The first challenge where to get it. I first learned this technique from veteran modeler Lou Sassi, who effectively "mined" the rust from an old automobile. I had a foot-long section of steel rail that had sat neglected in my garage for several years. It had rusted, and I was able to gather pieces that had fallen off in thin layers, which is ideal.

Once we have the rust, we need to make it useable. Larger pieces can be suitable for parts of loads or for junkyard scenes, looking like random rusted components. I took some of the larger pieces and crushed them with the blunt plastic handle of a tool. Once that was done, I sifted them so I had a variety: fine powder, small rubble, and larger pieces.

Keep safety in mind when doing this. You're dealing with fine pieces of metal, and you don't want any to get in your eyes (or nose or mouth), and you don't want to get cut by a jagged piece. Wear safety goggles and a face mask when using these techniques.

Start by giving the car floor a heavy coat of dark rust-colored paint. I used a wide brush to apply dark brown flat acrylic craft paint. While it is still wet, add the pieces of rust on top of the paint. When the paint dries, it will hold the rust in place.

You can take this effect to any level you desire. You can do it in small patches using fine rust powder. I wanted a lot of fragments in this car, so I simply poured the whole container I'd prepped in place, then used a brush to push it around to make sure the floor was thoroughly covered. This ranged from fine powder to larger pieces.

When the paint was dry, I dumped any still-loose pieces onto a sheet of paper and poured them back into my rust container for future use. Remember that rust is conductive and magnetic, so we don't want stray metal bits coming out of the car later to cause wiring and track issues. A small flake of rust lodged in a turnout can easily cause a short circuit that would be tough to troubleshoot.

To fix this, I sealed the rust in place the same way I treat scenery. I started by wetting it with rubbing alcohol, applied by a pipette. I followed by dribbling it with thinned matte medium (3:1 water to matte medium). Even though I was careful, this left a puddle in the bottom of the car; I used a paper towel to wick up the excess a couple of times. Once it dries, the rust is securely in place.

Another option is to paint the floor varied colors depending upon its simulated surface, whether it's supposed to be wood planks or sheet steel (see what Cody Grivno did to create a realistic steel floor on page 60). For gons with wood plank flooring, see the following sections on flatcar decks for ideas.

To weather both the interior walls and exterior sides and ends, I used oil-paint washes. As Chapter 3 described, I put small dots of various rust-color oil paints on a piece of plastic, wet a wide, flat brush in turpentine, and streaked it vertically until I had the effects I was looking for.

Oil paints are forgiving, allowing multiple attempts to get the streaks exactly where I wanted. Once that was done, I let the car dry several days before giving it a clear flat finish.

The underbody and trucks were painted in various rust and grime colors, as described in Chapter 4.

I weathered the gondola's interior walls (top), as well as the sides (bottom), with washes of rust-colored oil paints. Dip the brush in turpentine, then touch the bristle tips to the paint (on the card in the background) and streak it on the car. Oil paints provide lots of working time.

FLATCARS

Flatcars are prime candidates for weathering, as — like gondolas — their decks are out in the open, easy to see, and haul a variety of heavy, bulky products that often leave scars behind from the loading and unloading processes.

Flatcars come in many styles and variations, including general-purpose cars, cars with bulkheads, and specialty cars such as piggyback and container flatcars and center-beam lumber cars. As with other cars, the best way to obtain a realistic appearance is to look at prototype examples, then figure out the best way to duplicate the effects.

A key difference among flatcars is whether they have a wood deck or steel

This HO Proto 2000 car has a plastic deck, molded in gray, with simulated wood grain and bolt details. A few layers of paint and washes made the deck look much more like the real thing.

Roughing up the deck gave it a more realistic texture and also gave the weathering paints a better surface to adhere to. I started with coarse sandpaper (top) and moved on to a razor saw (bottom).

deck. General-purpose cars often have wood decks, while others are steel; a further variation on wood decks is whether they started out painted or were simply treated lumber (using creosote or other preservative).

A modeling variation for wood decks is whether the wood planks are represented with real wood or injection-molded plastic with molded-in woodgrain texture, fastener detail, and board separations.

SOO LINE FLATCAR

A common challenge with flatcars (and many gons as well) is making injection-molded plastic look like wood. This HO Proto 2000 flatcar is a good candidate, as it is a nice model with a sharp paint job, but the gray plastic deck needed some help. Here's how I did it.

The deck boards have simulated woodgrain and bolt-head detail, which was nice, but I gave the deck some additional texture. I started with 120-grit sandpaper, rubbed lengthwise to the boards. I then scraped a razor along the boards and also added some gouges lengthwise along the deck. I finished by using a dental pick to add some more deep gouges.

These treatments do a couple of things. It kills any plastic shine — a dull surface will hold weathering paint better — and it makes it look like the car has been in service for a while, hauling loads that have scarred the deck.

For color, I wanted to represent a deck with treated lumber that had been in service for several years. This type of wood usually starts out close to black, but fades to dark and medium gray, often with streaks of dark and medium brown depending upon age.

I painted the deck in layers, starting with a multi-color wash. I put several drops of black, brown, and gray acrylic paint on a piece of plastic, then swirled the paint together to create a larger color variety.

I dipped a wide, flat brush into water, then touched it to the paint and streaked it across the deck, repeating the process with different colors to give individual boards a varied appearance. When that dried, I painted and drybrushed some boards with heavier doses of color. I also made sure that the ends of the boards were painted. When that dried, I gave the whole deck a light wash of thinned black.

The rest of the car was straightforward. I painted the trucks and underframe a mix of dark brown and dark gray, then used oil-paint washes down the sides of the car using various rust colors.

BULKHEAD FLAT

I found a yellow Trailer Train bulkhead flatcar (next page) lurking in a yard on Kalmbach's HO Milwaukee, Racine & Troy staff layout. It's an old Roundhouse (Model Die Casting) kit that had been given a quick, basic dust-colored weathering overspray years ago, and then placed in service. I wanted to give it a bit more detailed weathering job; it's a good example of what you can do with a simple kit.

This flatcar is typical of those running from the 1970s to today. Prototype cars of this type have either wood or steel decks and bulkhead walls; this one is a combination, with a simulated wood deck (painted yellow), with smooth interior bulkhead walls, representing steel.

I started with the deck, painting it to represent a prototype wood deck that had been painted the car color but was starting to wear after a few years

I gave the deck a multi-color wash. I wet the brush, dipped the bristles into various dark grays and browns, and streaked the deck side-to-side.

When the initial wash was dry, I painted and drybrushed individual boards varying colors ranging from black to light brown to simulate aged, treated wood.

The flatcar sides received washes of various brown oil colors, streaked downward, to simulate rust and grime.

This bulkhead flat (an HO Roundhouse model) received some physical distressing to the deck, followed by washes and drybrushing.

After sanding and gouging the deck, I gave it a wash of thinned black craft paint. This was followed by drybrushing individual boards various shades of dark gray.

To simulate wear on the steel bulkheads, I made a few gouges with a dental pick, added brown oil colors (with a toothpick as shown here), then created streaks under them with a brush dampened in turpentine.

of service. I treated it the same way as with the Soo Line car, roughing up the deck with coarse sandpaper and a razor saw. You can distress it to whatever extent you desire.

I followed this with a wash of black craft paint thinned with alcohol. This accentuated the seams between boards as well as any gouges and scrapes that I'd created. Next was a combination of drybrushing and washes of dark brown and grimy black colors, giving some boards a heavier treatment, followed by another grimy black wash over the deck.

The bulkhead walls can take a beating from loads that shift as well as from getting dinged by various products as they're being loaded and unloaded. I used a dental pick to create a couple of gouges in each end. A toothpick worked well for adding dark brown oil paint into a couple of the gouges to simulate rust, followed by a brush wet with turpentine to streak the colors downward. I also added a couple of small rust spots with the same technique atop the bulkheads.

I finished the car by streaking its sides with various browns and blacks and giving the ends a wash of grimy black. The resulting car still looks new-ish, but you can tell it's been in service for a few years.

PIGGYBACK CARS

Steel-deck flatcars weather differently than their wood-decked cousins. I based the weathering on this former Accurail HO flush-deck car and Walthers channel-side car based on prototype photos I'd taken.

I gave the decks of both cars a light airbrushed coat of thinned white to simulate the paint fading. To match specific prototypes, I added new Details West trailer hitches: an American Car & Foundry Model 5 in the middle of the Accurail car and a TT-2 hitches on the Walthers car.

The flush-deck car represents an all-purpose (container or piggyback) car that has built-in container pedestals that can be moved along channels along the outside of the deck. I added a black wash to these areas to accentuate the channel/slot openings.

On both cars, I painted several small patches of brown and dark gray

Prototype piggyback cars receive a lot of wear on their decks, plus paint fading from exposure to the elements. This is an all-purpose (container/piggyback) car; the slots along the edge of the deck hold container pedestals.

These HO 89-foot piggyback cars received a mix of airbrush oversprays and painted-on rust, grime, and wear effects. The flush-deck car (rear) was produced by Accurail; the channel-side car is from Walthers.

acrylic paints to simulate areas where the surface had been dinged and was forming rust. I also added a larger rust patch in the middle of the Walthers cars. I used my finger to rub dark gray chalk on areas where trailer tires would have left wear marks on the deck, then accented several areas with rust-color PanPastels.

I finished by giving the decks of each a light overspray of thinned black, then drybrushed grimy black and brown paints down the sides of each.

The molded channels and container-pedestal slots along each side of the flush-deck car received two coats of black wash. I had to later touch up a few areas where the wash escaped the recessed area.

A makeup sponge worked well to apply dabs of rust-colored PanPastels around the earlier washes and acrylic-paint rust areas.

RUSTED STEEL GONDOLA FLOOR

Cody Grivno applied a variety of weathering effects in layers to create this realistically rusted steel gondola floor in HO scale. Cody Grivno

Cody Grivno captured the appearance of a rusted steel gondola floor by layering effects. He started by spraying the interior with a dark red (Tamiya Red Brown) and followed with a coat of Testor's Dullcote.

He then took advantage of the reactive properties of alcohol and Dullcote by applying a layer of Monroe Models Quick Age Weathering Wash (No. 978), which is alcohol-based, with a brush. He then used a small piece of foam held in tweezers to blot up some of the wash, resulting in a mottled appearance, which is appropriate since flooring rarely weathers uniformly.

Once that was dry, he used a 10-0 paintbrush to add Monroe's Dark Rust Weathering Wash (No. 979), letting it flow just into the seams between the flooring panels and around other details to accentuate them.

REAL WOOD FLATCAR DECK

One way of dealing with the plastic simulated-wood deck on a flatcar is to replace it with a real wood deck. You can use stripwood cut to length and glued in place, or you can swap in a commercial laser-cut deck, as I did here. The car is an HO Proto 2000 50-foot flatcar, and the deck is a one-piece part from American Model Builders.

Once the deck was in place, I gave the boards random washes of several colors, including black, grimy black, and shades of brown. When that dried, I went over the car again, drybrushing several boards with these colors and following with progressively darker washes.

I began the weathering on this real wood deck (a laser-cut part from AMB) with paint and washes on individual boards using black, grimy black, and several shades of brown.

Washes of dark gray finished the deck. Apply washes in light coats, building up effects slowly and letting each wash dry thoroughly; washes on wood typically look darker when initially applied than when they're dry.

REAL CEMENT ON A COVERED HOPPER

Although this is a closed car, it provides a good example of how a simulated load spill can show what type of service the car is in. Mont Switzer started with an HO Kadee two-bay cement hopper, using real cement to model the spill. He opened the hatches, then brushed a heavy coat of Testor's Dullcote around the hatches (clear acrylic flat would work as well). Mont then used a Popsicle stick to scoop some cement, then sprinkle and brush it over the Dullcote. The excess can be brushed away after it dries. Mont notes that the cement will appear dark at first, but become lighter once it's dry.

Mont weathered the rest of the car with conventional methods, using weathering powders to capture the overall gray, dusty look typical of prototype cars used in cement service.

Cement-service covered hoppers have an overall gray, dusty look, with spills often apparent on the roof. Mont Switzer copied this appearance in HO by using real cement. Two photos: Mont Switzer

Clear flat finish brushed around the hatches served as a binder to hold the cement powder in place.

Weathering effects on this Atlas HO switcher included chalk grime on the sides, trucks, and pilot; drybrushed rust and grime on the cab roof, hood roof, and sides of the frame; a rust patch and streaks on the exhaust stack; and a black wash in the radiator grill and hood-door louvers, which show nicely against the white lettering. Since there's no cab interior, I wasn't picky about letting the cab windows get frosted a bit from the clear flat coat that sealed the weathering.

CHAPTER SEVEN

Diesel locomotives

The expanding use of diesel locomotives in the 1940s and 1950s brought an explosion of colorful paint schemes not seen on steam locomotives. However, in spite of the bright colors and sharp designs, even locomotives that had only been in service a short time would begin to show signs of weathering.

This SD40-2 has been recently repainted by BNSF prior to this 2006 photo, but it still shows weathering effects: namely a healthy coat of dust on the trucks, fuel tank (especially on the end), and pilot.

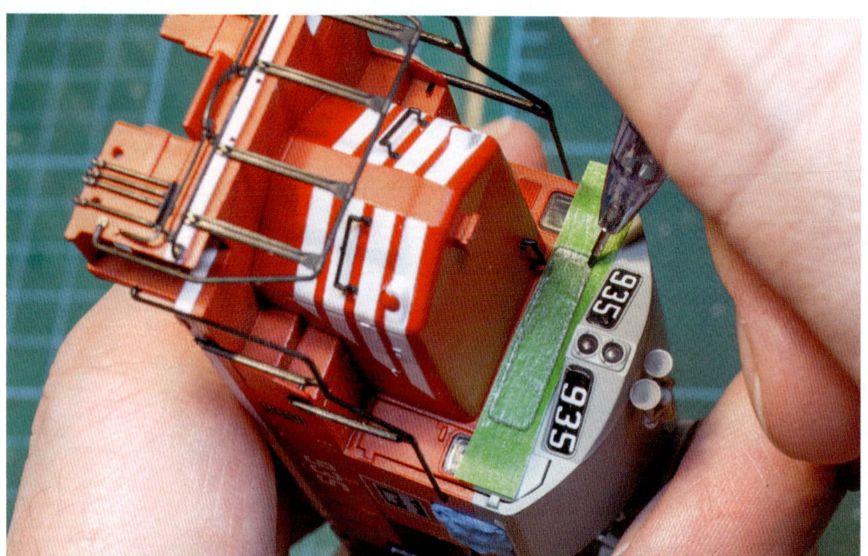

Mask windows of diesels prior to weathering. You can use masking tape (top; tracing with a pencil allows cutting an accurate pattern) or a piece of poster putty (bottom), pressed to the proper shape.

A key difference between weathering and wear on locomotives compared to freight cars is that, unlike freight cars, locomotives are periodically cleaned and repainted. Some railroads washed locomotives on a regular basis; this was especially true of passenger locomotives through the 1960s. Other railroads weren't as fastidious, and the only time their diesels were thoroughly cleaned was following major repairs. Since railroads varied widely in their approaches to this, use prototype photos as your reference, and follow the typical practices of the railroad you model.

Weathering effects on locomotives are a combination of soot from exhaust; dirt, sand, and grime kicked up from the track and roadbed; fuel stains; rust patches from wear or damage and resulting streaks and stains; and aging effects, such as paint that bleaches, fades, and peels, and lettering that fades or runs.

Another common effect — especially since the 1990s — is patched-out painting and restenciling for locomotives that have been sold to other railroads or leasing companies. This is sometimes done neatly, but sometimes hurriedly and sloppily.

PREP AND FLAT FINISH

If you have detail parts to add or modify (snowplows, antennas, uncoupling levers, horns, hoses, etc.), do it before adding any weathering. Also, do any needed detail painting, such as grab irons, handrails, steps, air hoses, and horns.

Out of the box, diesel locomotive models typically have semigloss or gloss finishes, with lettering that's likewise glossy. As with freight cars, our first job is to give the model a flat finish to eliminate the shine and provide a good base for weathering effects.

Because locomotives have more nooks and crannies than typical freight cars, the best way to get an even flat finish is by spraying, either with a rattle can or airbrush. My preference is an airbrush; I usually wait until I have several models needing attention so I can do them all at once. Most of the locomotives in this chapter were given a coat of Model Master Acryl flat finish, thinned 50/50 with its thinner.

Unless we're going for a special effect, we don't want our window glazing coated with clear flat (which will look dirty or foggy). There are a couple of options in dealing with it. The usual solution is to mask the glazing prior to applying the flat finish. You can do this with masking tape: Press a piece over the windshield area, outline it with a pencil, and then remove the tape and cut the outline with a hobby knife or small scissors.

Another quick method is to use poster putty. Press a small blob of it over the glazing and use a toothpick to spread it to match the window area. Be careful not to press too hard, or you risk accidentally popping the glazing out of the opening.

With either technique, leave the masking in place until the weathering is complete and you've given the model a final clear flat coat. If you do get flat finish on the clear glazing, brushing the window with a couple of coats of clear gloss finish will restore its original appearance.

While you're doing this, you can add windshield-wiper effects to windshields by adding masking tape in the pattern that would be cleared by the wiper blades before adding the clear flat coat (see chapter 10 on vehicles for an example of this on an automobile).

For a windshield-wiper pattern/dirty windshield effect, cut masking tape to the pattern that would be cleared by the wiper blade and apply it before weathering and spraying with clear flat. You can touch up the area with clear gloss and a brush.

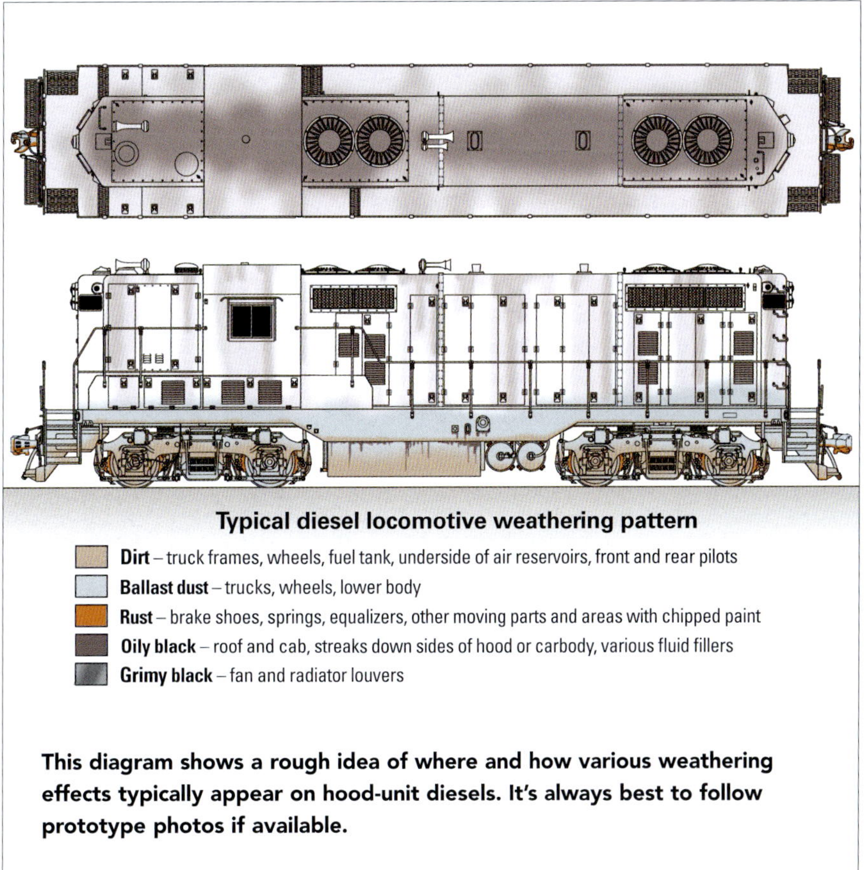

This diagram shows a rough idea of where and how various weathering effects typically appear on hood-unit diesels. It's always best to follow prototype photos if available.

Yet another option is to hand-paint the effect with clear gloss coat on the glazing after applying the clear flat coat.

Dust, grime, and soot are primary weathering effects on diesels; the extent of each varies by age, type of service, frequency of washing, and the base paint colors. The chart above shows typical locations for various types of weathering.

ROOFS AND EXHAUST STAINS

Among the first weathering that appears on a locomotive is soot from exhaust; even freshly shopped and cleaned locomotives will soon show its effects. This isn't always apparent when viewing trains from trackside, but look down from a bridge or other elevated vantage point and you'll quickly realize the extent of this effect.

Roofs quickly acquire a coat of dark soot from exhaust. This is an Amtrak Genesis locomotive viewed from a bridge.

Chalks are great for capturing exhaust soot effects. Here Cody Grivno is adding Monroe Models grimy black chalk to the roof of an N scale Kato ES44AC. The final effect will be a bit lighter once excess chalk is blown away and a clear flat finish is applied. Cody Grivno

Exhaust stains are initially concentrated around the exhaust stacks and fans on the roof, but over time the entire roof will take on a dark, grungy appearance of dark gray to near black. Streaks may appear as rain washes some of the soot downward and to the side. This is most noticeable on rounded surfaces, such as the arched roofs on cab units, some switchers, and on locomotive cab roofs.

Locomotives on railroads operating in the mountains, where engines work hard within tunnels, will often show heavier exhaust effects over the whole body than those of flatlands railroads.

Because exhaust effects are feathered, usually without distinct edges, they're best simulated by powdered chalks or thinned oversprays applied with an airbrush. For chalks, you may have to layer multiple coats with clear flat finish to get a heavier effect.

Use dark gray to black chalk or paint for this, but if you're weathering a black locomotive, a medium gray will help bring out the details of the roof (and also simulate a bleached-paint appearance typical of darkly painted roofs).

Here's Cody's finished model, with an unweathered version to show the extent of the weathering. Cody also added dust-colored chalk on the trucks and lower body, a black wash to the grills, and spot color on various details. The weathering really adds depth and highlights the model's details. Cody Grivno

The exhaust stacks themselves take a beating from the high temperatures to which they're exposed. Paint the insides flat black to give them depth. Streaking the outsides vertically with rust and dark gray will give them an aged appearance, with possibly some grime or rust streaks extending farther from the stack toward the sides.

SCREENS, FANS, AND LOUVERS

Diesels have a variety of screened, grilled, and louvered openings on their sides, with fan openings and grills atop the roof. How you treat them will vary by the quality of the model's molding and the base color of the body at the grill. Most prototype grills and screens are painted to match the body; others are galvanized, a dull metallic gray color.

The grill moldwork on many earlier diesel models was rather basic, with simple raised patterns to simulate the grill or grid. Most newer models have finer, more detailed molding, often with multilayer effects. With any of these, you can usually improve their appearance by adding a black wash to the area. The wash will settle into the recessed areas, providing depth. If you find the wash has crept out of the recesses as it dried, you can clean up the adjoining area by rubbing it with a pencil eraser or toothpick, or by adding a bit of touch-up paint.

The photo of the Illinois Central diesel on page 69 shows further weathering in these areas. Oil-bath filters or filters that become dirty can leave stains tracing downward. These can be simulated with grimy black drybrushing, washes, and PanPastels. The IC locomotive also illustrates how these weathering effects stand out much more on light-color paint schemes.

Do this to simple louvers as well. You can see the effects of giving washes to louvers over lettering on the Burlington engine on page 62, giving the louvers a more distinct appearance.

TRUCKS AND WHEELS

Locomotive trucks show weathering effects fairly quickly after painting or shopping. As the wheels turn, they

BOW-WAVE AND OTHER EFFECTS

A common weathering effect on cab units was for a dust and grime pattern that starts just behind the pilot and feathers upward and rearward starting above the lead truck, called the "bow-wave" effect. It's shown in the prototype image of the Gulf, Mobile & Ohio E unit, with lighter-colored dust starting heavily above the truck and becoming lighter as it progresses down the side.

I've re-created the effect with powdered chalk on this HO Athearn Genesis-series F unit decorated for Missouri Pacific. Other effects on the model include painted and drybrushed grime and rust streaks and oil stain on the fuel tank; chalked soot on the roof; dust- and rust-color chalk on the trucks; drybrushed streaks of rust and grime on the exhaust stacks and on the roof next to them, and simulated wiper patterns on the windshield (see page 65). I also added some light gray streaks on the handrails next to the cab door to show wear.

As with other models, I sealed the chalk effects with a light coat of acrylic clear flat, applied with an airbrush.

The "bow wave" effect was common on cab units, where dust and sand was kicked up by the lead truck and feathered upward behind the pilot. Chalk accomplished this on the HO Missouri Pacific Athearn model (top). The effect is quite apparent on the lead E7 on the Gulf, Mobile & Ohio passenger train (bottom). Prototype photo: J. David Ingles

EXTREME WEATHERING

The paint on this prototype Union Pacific SD40-2 is definitely showing its age in the 2007 photo above, with the yellow and gray both fading in patches. There's significant grime accumulation, along with rust streaks and patches, on the trucks, tank, and other components.

Cody Grivno effectively modeled these effects using an N scale Kato SD40-2 as a starting point. Cody mixed light versions of paint (acrylic white mixed with UP yellow and UP gray) and used a brush to apply it in patches. Cody took the effects even further, adding painted rust colors along the roofline, dynamic brake grid, tank, lower body, and trucks. He simulated peeling lettering by painting patches over the factory letters.

After adding additional drybrushed grime effects on the roof, tank, and trucks, Cody finished the model with an overspray of very thin white acrylic paint.

The paint on many of Union Pacific's SD40-2s weathered to multiple shades of gray and yellow, as shown at top. Cody Grivno captured this by mixing white with the locomotive colors and painting it in patches (below). Model photo: Cody Grivno

kick up grime and dirt from the track and from the roadbed. In addition, locomotives use sand for traction. This light-colored sand is blown through a small pipe ahead of the wheels, and as the wheels rotate, they crush the sand to a powder that blows throughout the sideframe. These effects will be more pronounced on mainline locomotives working trains on steep grades, and with switchers and other locomotives working in yards.

Model truck frames are usually black engineering plastic. Brush-painting them with a coat of grimy black is a good start; you can also mix in lighter gray or brown/rust colors to match specific prototypes. You can air-brush them, as well.

Chalk is very effective for simulating dust and grime on trucks, as it's easy to work among the crevices of the sideframe details. I generally use a mix of medium gray and dark rust colors, but if I'm modeling a specific locomotive I'll try to match what I see — which may be a buff or sand color. Colors vary widely depending on the type of service, the type of soil in the area, and the type of sand used for traction.

Wheel faces should be painted a shade of medium to dark brown for locomotives with roller-bearing trucks (most diesels since the mid-1940s). Some switchers had solid-bearing trucks, relying on grease in journal boxes for lubricating axle ends; these can have wheels that are darker shades of gray or black, with a shiny appearance from the grease that often found its way to the wheels. Follow the same guidelines as with freight cars.

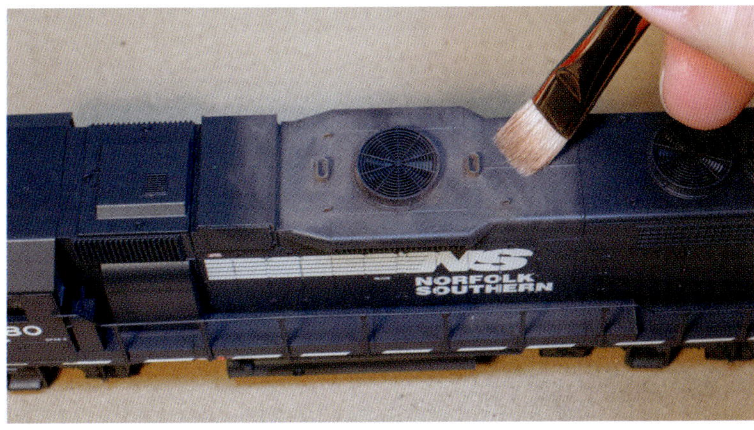

On black models, a lighter shade of gray will accentuate details and help simulate the bleaching effect that occurs on dark paint from exposure to sunlight. The prototype photo at right shows a Norfolk Southern diesel in distributed-power service. Prototype photo: Mark Watson

A wash of thinned black paint works well for simulating depth in grills, screens, and louvers. This is thinned acrylic craft paint.

Weathering effects are more pronounced on light-colored diesels. This Illinois Central engine shows dark grills with grime streaking down from them, and the louvered vents are quite pronounced. Note the overall coating of grime.

Applying a black wash over the louvers creates depth on the lettered areas of this black switcher. You can see the final effects, with additional weathering added, in the photo on page 62.

Most model truck frames are shiny black engineering plastic. Start by painting them a mix of grimy black and brown colors. Use prototype photos, found in books and on railfan websites, as a guide for colors.

Powdered chalk works well for simulating dust and grime effects on trucks. If you have an airbrush, thinned oversprays also work well. Follow prototype photos.

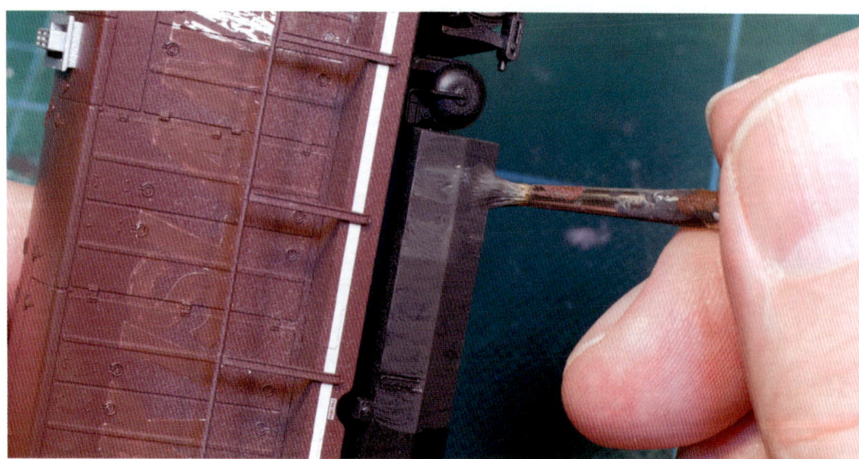

As with the trucks, paint fuel tanks a mix of grimy black, dark gray, and brown. Using a brush helps show the streaks that are often apparent on prototype locomotives. The lettering effects are shown in Chapter 9.

FUEL TANKS

Fuel tanks acquire distinctive weathering patterns. Take care of detailing and detail painting this area as needed first. The emergency fuel cutoff has a red housing, and the cap on the fuel filler pipe is red. If the tank color is black — the most common prototype color — a good step is to paint it a lighter shade of grimy black, dark gray, and dark brown (or combinations of those colors) with a brush.

Since the tank rides right above the track between the trucks, the ends of the tank in particular acquire lots of grime and splatter from the wheels. Chalk and washes in various dirt and grime shades will capture this.

Many tanks show streaks of spilled diesel fuel, which usually shows as a slightly shiny, darker area that has acquired additional dirt. In simulating fuel spills, remember than diesel fuel is not black. It takes a pretty heavy spill (or repeated small ones) to look black, and this color is usually the result of the fuel's glossier appearance and its attracting dirt and grime.

For modeling fuel-tank spills I prefer Polly Scale oily black, which isn't black; it's a brownish color that will leave a slightly shiny streak behind, just like a real spill. For a darker effect, paint a bit of grimy black first, then follow with a coat of oily black. See the Missouri Pacific F unit on page 67 as an example.

PILOTS

Locomotive pilots often weather quickly and heavily, as they're subject to grime and dirt kicked up by neighboring wheels. They also get dinged by small rocks and other debris at speed, often leading to marks and small patches of rust.

Start with detail painting of the MU hoses and connectors, uncoupling lever, coupler, and any other details. You can then add weathering using a combination of chalks, washes, oversprays, and painted-on rust patches to achieve various effects.

GENERAL EFFECTS

Overall dust and grime effects can be simulated with chalk dusting,

PanPastels, thinned oversprays, or a combination of techniques. Keep an eye out for patterns that form on certain types of locomotives, and how certain prototype paint colors and schemes weather.

An example is with cab units, where dust and dirt tends to be heaviest on the sides just behind the pilot and above the lead truck, with the effect tapering and feathering upward and rearward along the side. Called the "bow wave" effect, this can sometimes be seen to lesser extremes on hood units, where the recessed sides limit the effect (see page 67).

Other general weathering and highlights can include:

• Door latches: Hood and cab door latches can be highlighted with a gray or rust-colored artist's pencil.

• Handrails: These are painted on most newer models; older models sometimes have unpainted black plastic or bare metal rails. Paint these appropriate colors. Railings at the corner

On pilots, highlight details with spot colors: Grimy black for hoses, light gray or flat silver for glad hands and air valves, appropriate colors for grab irons and handrails, and brown for rust on the coupler. Cody Grivno also gave this Dakota, Minnesota & Eastern HO model an overspray of thinned grimy black, with brown areas painted and drybrushed to represent small rust patches. Cody Grivno

Some weathering effects are railroad-specific. The BNSF had extreme fading issues with the orange paint on some of its locomotives, as on this Dash 9-44CW in 2007. The contrast is quite noticeable with the replaced equipment panel behind the cab and the trailing locomotive.

PATCHOUTS AND REPAIRS

Older locomotives are sometimes repaired using body parts from other locomotives that might not match, just as an old car might get a fender that's a different color from the scrapyard. The most common details for this are hood-unit engine compartment doors (many of which are interchangeable), fan hatches (which are usually modular), battery-box doors, and side panels on cab units.

You can often re-create this simply by repainting the part, perhaps in primer gray, a color used in another of the railroad's paint schemes, or by a fresh coat of the accurate color applied after weathering the locomotive. The ex-SP model at right bears a yellow panel from a UP donor locomotive painted in its new owner's colors.

As with freight cars, locomotives coming off of their initial lease agreements (often at their 15- or 20-year birthdays) were often resold to other railroads or leasing companies. Although these were sometimes repainted, it's common for the new owner to only do a quick paintout of the original

Following Chicago & North Western's merger into Union Pacific, the UP used its own Armour Yellow to paint out the C&NW logo and roadname on this SD40-2, followed by its own decal numbers and nose logo.

steps are usually a contrasting color for visibility; check the prototype for the right color. You can also add grime and wear spots at high-use locations next to steps.

• General rust patches: These can be painted with acrylic or oil paints, with the resulting streaks drybrushed. This simulates dings and scrapes along the frame, on the pilots, or on the nose and rear.

• Traction sand spills: Simulate with chalk on and near filler hatch locations.

• Battery boxes: These sometimes show light streaks from battery leakage. Their most common location on hood units is just forward of the cab, atop the walkway.

HEAVY WEATHERING

Locomotives that remain in service for several years without repainting will exhibit more and more extreme weathering effects as they age. These effects will vary in type and intensity based on the type of service and environment and the quality of the original paint (and in many cases the order in which paint coats or various colors are layered). See "Extreme weathering" on page 68.

Peeling lettering is a common effect. This can be partial peeling of lettering large herald or roadname, plus a patchout of the locomotive number on the cab.

Variations of this happened with mergers, as well. At a merger, locomotives of the merged railroad were sometimes painted right away, but sometimes this process took several years. Renumbering was often fast, however. Southern Pacific and Chicago & North Western diesels with their road numbers painted out and new Union Pacific-style numbers in place were common when those railroads were merged.

Kim Nipkow replicated this as shown in the model photo below, starting with a Kato C44-9W HO model factory-painted for SP. Kim applied various weathering effects in layers, including chalk, washes, and weathering sprays. He then sprayed yellow patches — including the number and nose logo patchouts and the simulated new equipment box cover behind the cab, applied decals (Microscale 87-523), then some final weathering touchup and flat clear coat.

Kim Nipkow nicely captured the appearance of a patched-out former Southern Pacific locomotive starting with a stock SP-painted HO Kato C44-9W. Kim Nipkow

or logos, or letters completely disappearing. It can be simulated by painting the body color over the lettering (if the shade varies slightly, that's OK; it simulates the color difference between faded, exposed paint and the paint that's been hidden by the lettering paint. Chapter 9 shows some examples and how to model them.

Body paint sometimes fades over time. This is especially true with some lighter colors (particularly oranges, yellows, and reds), and some railroads' schemes are notorious for bleaching and fading. The orange used on early BNSF locomotives, for example, often faded to a bleached, light color, as seen on page 71.

This fading can be re-created in several ways, as with the freight cars in earlier chapters. You can try dusting the model with white chalk. This will produce a faded effect, but the results can vary depending upon the body color involved. You can layer the effect by sealing the chalk with a light coat of clear flat and repeating the chalk.

An overspray of thinned white or light gray paint, applied with an airbrush, will allow more control of the effect. If you're trying to fade only one body color, you may want to mask other colors first.

I weathered this Rock Island 0-6-0 switcher, a ready-to-run HO Proto 2000 model, as if it were reaching the end of its 30-plus-year career in the early 1950s. A key to weathering steam is light colors that bring out details; effects on this model include chalks, PanPastels, drybrushing, washes, detail painting, and thinned oversprays.

CHAPTER EIGHT

Steam locomotives

Steam locomotives were usually black, a color that we've learned largely disappears in our modeled world. However, steam locomotives' unique weathering patterns are distinctive, and capturing these features effectively will bring out details and greatly improve realism.

This Norfolk & Western 0-8-0, shown in the late 1950s, is a fairly clean locomotive, but many weathering effects are still visible, including grime and dust on the running gear, streaks on the boiler, and rust and grime on the front and pilot.
Richard Jay Solomon

Even in this black-and-white photo, it's obvious that this "black" Missouri Pacific 2-8-4 really isn't black. The running gear is light from sand and dust, the tender sides have light streaks, numbers are partially coated, the boiler shows streaks in front of the cab, and there's a grungy appearance at the smokebox and down through the cylinders. *Trains* magazine collection

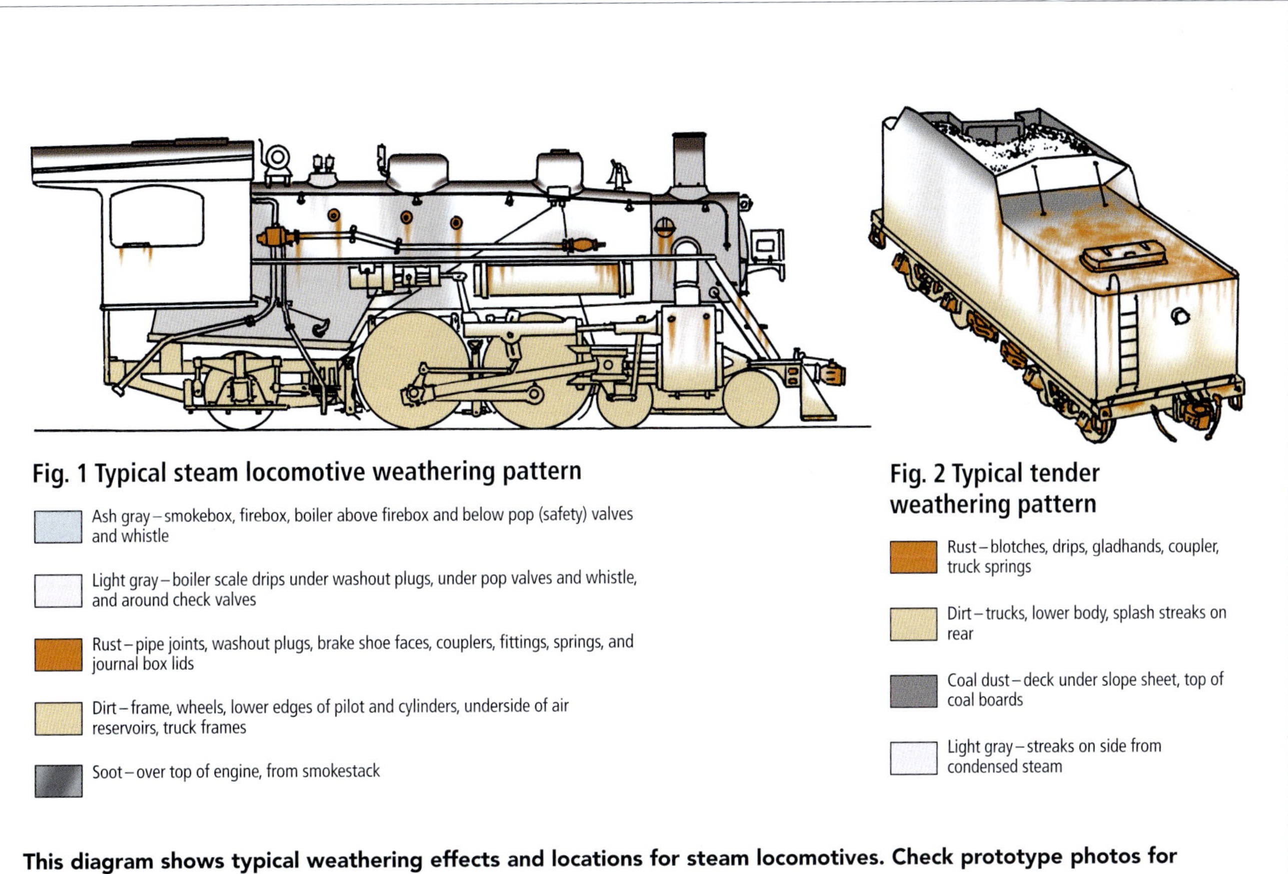

This diagram shows typical weathering effects and locations for steam locomotives. Check prototype photos for examples whenever possible. Kalmbach Media

It can be a challenge to accurately model steam weathering effects simply because the locomotives are no longer around to provide inspiration. They've been gone from mainline service in the U.S. since the late 1950s. Also, most photo coverage of them is in black and white, which doesn't show their many color nuances.

Although some still operate at museums and in excursion service, those locomotives are usually kept in pristine condition — unlike a heavy freight-service locomotive — so they don't necessarily provide the examples we're looking for.

The upper left photo (opposite) shows a nice color example of a steam switcher. Even with black-and-white images (lower left), you can often see weathering patterns and streaks that provide guidelines for modeling.

Let's take a look at how steam locomotives weathered the way they did, and what we can do to capture those effects in model form.

WEATHERING PATTERNS

Steam locomotives worked in a physical environment made difficult by their very operation. If you've seen a steam locomotive working up close, you know they produce an incredible amount of smoke and soot.

Now picture several of these locomotives working in close quarters and working in and through tight areas such as tunnels, passenger terminals, yards, and engine terminals, and you'll understand why the pervasive weathering effect on steam locomotives is that of grungy, dark-gray soot from smoke, along with coal dust, which was kicked up in small clouds every time a tender was loaded.

Oil-burning locomotives were not immune, as they could also produce a tremendous amount of smoke. Oil-fired locomotives burned a thick, sludgy product called "Bunker C" (now called No. 6 fuel oil), which required heating to get it to flow, and it did not burn very cleanly.

Along with smoke, steam locomotives had lots of visible moving parts, all of which required oil and grease lubrication, which left traces around many components. Evaporating water left behind mineral deposits, which were often apparent on areas such as the boiler, cylinders, whistle, and the top and sides of the tender. Dust from emptying the ash pan — required on a frequent basis — and dust from traction sand ground up by driving wheels coated the running gear and underside of the locomotive and tender.

All of the above weathering effects tend to gather on and around specific areas. The drawing above shows typical wear and weathering patterns on a steam locomotive, and it provides a good starting point when weathering a model.

You can use a wide variety of techniques to weather steam locomotives, including paint and paint washes, chalk, drybrushing, and PanPastels. As with any other model, you can take it

From the box, the Proto 2000 model shows nice detail, but the black finish and bright running gear are quite unrealistic. The biggest challenges will be toning down the silver areas and the shiny metal of the wheels and rods. I've just given the boiler and cab a quick brush-painting of acrylic clear flat.

It's difficult to see much inside of steam locomotive cabs. If your model has cab interior detail, kill any plastic shine with a coat of flat grimy black. Highlight gauges, valves, and handles with lighter colors — the goal is just to provide the impression of an interior.

to any level you'd like depending upon the age of the locomotive and the type of service its in.

Steam locomotives in passenger service, especially on first-class name trains into the 1950s, were frequently washed and kept in better appearance than other locomotives. This includes most steam locomotives that were not painted black: examples include Southern's green locomotives, Milwaukee Road's orange-and-gray *Hiawatha* engines, New York Central's gray Hudsons, and Southern Pacific's *Daylight* orange and red locomotives.

Most steam locomotives, however, were painted basic black. It was cheap and visually the best choice for hiding the pervasive soot and coal dust the engines inevitably acquired.

As with diesels and freight cars, start by making sure your model has a dead-flat finish. My subject model (a Proto 2000 HO scale Rock Island United States Railroad Administration-design 0-6-0 switcher) is pretty typical of modern steam models: It has nice detailing, with many separate details and piping. I wanted the model to represent an older locomotive in its last year of service.

Out of the box it simply looks too new, especially the shiny metal wheels, rods, and valve-gear components. The silver of the smokebox and firebox will also need to be toned down, as will the shiny plastic of the piping and detail parts. These are all common challenges with modeling steam, and they're easily fixed with weathering.

BOILER AND SMOKEBOX

The smokebox at the front of the boiler is subject to extreme heat. Some railroads painted this area black (in which case you can weather it the same as the boiler), but many railroads painted the smokebox with a mixture of graphite in oil. When fresh, this has a metallic gray appearance; exposure to heat, smoke, and soot over time turns it darker and darker.

Model manufacturers usually choose silver for this, which typically looks too bright to match the real thing. You can either paint the area with medium to dark gray, mixed with bit of silver to give it the look of graphite. The easiest solution is usually to just weather the silver area. I did this by streaking black downward with washes and drybrushing. I also brushed on dark gray chalk; a thinned grimy black overspray would work as well. This applies to the smokebox front, as well.

Atop the smokebox is the exhaust stack. Paint its interior flat black. The stack itself will be stained dark from smoke; do this with washes, drybrushing, and chalk. I used a brush and a mix of grimy black, gray, and dark brown paint to coat the visible piping, grab irons, bell and whistle cords, and compressor.

Atop the boiler are the sandbox (sand dome), steam dome, whistle, bell, and dynamo (generator). Look for white or light gray staining from water condensation and evaporation around the steam dome and dynamo (drybrushing) and sand dust around the sandbox (chalk or drybrushing).

The boiler itself has an overall cast of soot and smoke residue, which can include streaks. I added this with some grimy black and dark gray drybrushing, followed by dark gray chalks.

CAB AND FIREBOX

The level of detailing, access, and visibility of cab interiors vary widely among models. Many early and less expensive models have no cab interiors; often the motor protrudes into this space. Make sure these areas stay dark and hard to see on these models.

For models with cab interiors that are at least somewhat visible from the rear or through the side windows, details still probably won't be all that obvious. The goal is to paint and weather the interior just enough that it appears like the proper appliances are in there.

Paint the backhead and cab interior walls flat dark gray. You can then highlight individual details: light gray on gauges, red on valve handles, medium gray on the throttle and control levers.

The cab roof typically shows soot and smoke, and sometimes streaks of rust running crosswise. I added these with gray and brown drybrushing, PanPastels, and chalk. I also streaked

Black powdered chalk, applied with a stiff-bristle brush, works well to tone down the silver areas of the firebox and smokebox.

The most efficient way to evenly weather wheels and running gear is to airbrush the area with thinned gray and rust colors while wheels are slowly turning. Here Cody Grivno is weathering an HO Proto 2000 0-8-0. Do this in light layers. Jim Forbes

Rods and wheels can also be brush-painted, although you'll have to periodically rotate the wheels to ensure even coverage of all details.

I'm adding grime and rust streaks with gray and brown PanPastels and an applicator sponge on the Rock Island locomotive. I'll add additional light gray streaks to simulate mineral deposits near the water-fill hatch.

grime and rust colors down the cab sides, including over the locomotive number. Make sure the windows stay relatively clean.

Below and to the front of the cab, the lower part of the firebox and the ash pan can receive the same basic treatment as the boiler or smokebox, with drybrushing and chalk. This area was painted black on some locomotives and graphite on others; either way, they accumulated smoke, cinders, dust, and grime.

RUNNING GEAR

The running gear on steam models presents a challenge because of all the moving parts. For starters, paint everything on the frame itself (behind the drivers and under the cab) flat black to make it disappear. This is especially true on models where part of the motor or mechanical drive train is visible beneath the boiler.

A note on wheels: Many prototype steam locomotive portrait photos show driving wheels with white-painted rims. Understand that this was typically done for the benefit of the photographer for builder's portraits or other special occasions and was not standard practice on most railroads. Even if it was done on a new locomotive, the effect will quickly wear and weather, so painted rims are not common on locomotives that have been in service for any length of time.

The side rods, wheels, and valve gear quickly weather to a fairly uniform dark gray color, even though the rods start out a lighter gray. A great method to do this is to airbrush the running gear while it's in motion. You can do this on a temporary track placed in your spray booth. Apply low power and airbrush the running gear with a thinned mix of dark gray and brown while the wheels are turning slowly.

If you don't have an airbrush, you can use a brush to apply paint, washes, and PanPastels to the individual components. You'll have to apply power occasionally to move the rods and gear to get access to all areas.

On the valve gear and cylinders, the piston rod and crosshead hangers will be clean and lubricated from the motion of the moving parts. The cylinders will show grime and soot, and sometimes white or light-gray water-scale residue.

TENDER

Tenders are subjected to the same smoke and soot coatings as the locomotive, and — on coal burners — some extra coal dust added for good measure. This shows as an overall dark cast with streaks down the sides and rear, which often partially (and sometimes completely) obscures any lettering or logos.

You can combine effects to capture this. I used a mix of dark gray and brown drybrushing and PanPastels to create downward streaks, then added some light gray streaks on the sides near the water hatch to simulate mineral deposits from evaporated water spills. This area can show as a cleaner (darker) area where water overflow has washed some soot away. Check prototype photos for examples.

I added powdered black chalk to the tender sides to tone down the streaked effects and blend everything together. An overspray of thinned grimy black would work, as well. The tender deck received grime, soot, and rust effects from chalk and PanPastels. Seal all of the weathering effects with a light coat of clear flat.

If a tender has just been filled with water, there will be pools and puddles on the deck and around the hatch. You can capture the look of this by brushing acrylic clear gloss around and on the hatch and deck. Do this after all other weathering has been applied and sealed.

On oil-burning locomotives, like the Proto 2000 model, you'll often find spill stains on and near the fuel-filler hatch on the tender deck. This can be captured with a mix of dark gray paint or Polly Scale oily black, which I also applied after the chalk weathering was sealed.

Tender trucks can be treated much like freight car trucks (Chapter 4). Most had solid-bearing trucks with journal boxes, so dark gray sideframes are usually appropriate, with rust highlights with darker grease and oil stains

Water spills were common when filling the tender, leaving puddles and streaks on the tender deck. *Trains* magazine collection

You can simulate water spills and puddles by brushing acrylic clear gloss on the deck. Do this after applying all other weathering effects and the clear flat seal coat.

The finished tender deck shows various grime and rust patches, the spilled "water" near the hatch at right, and residue from oil spills at left, applied with Polly Scale oily black paint.

on the journal box lids and wheel faces.

Tenders on models of coal-burning models usually have the coal load simulated with a textured, molded plastic piece (or molded directly as part of the tender body), painted black with the tender. This can range from reasonably effective (if the molded texture is fine and detailed enough) to extremely unrealistic.

A relatively easy fix is to simply add a layer of scale coal over the load. To do this, paint a heavy coat of black plaint over the molded load, then sprinkle scale coal into the paint, press it in place, and let the paint dry overnight. Once it dries, dump out the excess and you're done.

You can also add additional coal to make a taller load; seal it by using an eyedropper to wet it with rubbing alcohol, then dribble diluted white glue over it in the same manner as ballasting track. Again, check prototype photos; some locomotives left engine terminals with very tall piles of coal in their bunkers.

OVERALL AND FINISHING

If any weathering has gotten on cab windows, headlights, and other "glass" areas, clean them off or refresh them with a brush and clear gloss finish (masking these areas with tape, as with diesels, is also a good idea). Areas like number boards will sometimes get wiped off if they get too grimy; you can simulate this, as well.

Other details across the locomotive that can receive detail paint and weathering effects include the pilot and couplers (treat them as with freight cars and diesels), piping, air hoses, pilot, and couplers.

With all of these effects, think in terms of layers and blending — and remember to start light and build up heavier effects gradually.

Ed Swain did a great job weathering this HO Pennsylvania Railroad Class I1 Decapod, a Broadway Limited Imports model. The engine is relatively clean, but has a coating of grime and dust across the running gear and lower tender. Note also the tall coal load he's added to the tender. Lou Sassi

4268
4268

CHAPTER NINE

"Ghost" and shadow lettering and paint

Among the more distinctive forms of weathering that develop on cars and locomotives, especially those that have been repainted at some point, is what's known as "ghost lettering." This can be shadows of lettering and logos where lettering has peeled away, or areas where a previous paint scheme is showing through the current paint job.

"Ghost" or "shadow" lettering comes in many forms. This Rock Island U33B is a factory-painted HO model from Atlas. It's lost most of its large billboard lettering to match a specific prototype. I've also given it a variety of drybrushed, airbrushed, and chalk effects, plus some washes.

Modeling these effects can be done in a number of ways. Some are relatively simple, some require a steady hand, and some involve complex layering of multiple effects, but all will result in distinctive, one-of-a kind models that will stand out on your layout.

We'll start with a relatively simple conversion, then move to some more complex projects.

ROCK ISLAND DIESEL

The Rock Island was known for its eclectic mix of motive power, which wore many schemes over the years. By the late 1960s and through the 1970s, the railroad's diesels tended to be heavily weathered, as the bankrupt railroad was having a hard enough time maintaining their diesels' components, much less their paint jobs.

The railroad's newer General Electric diesels originally wore a scheme of maroon with large side lettering. The letters, however, were not durable, and wore away after a few years of exposure to the elements, leaving behind shadowed patterns of the letters. The prototype photo on page 86 shows one of Rock's 10 U33Bs — acquired in 1969 — that had lost most of its side lettering by 1976. You can, however, see where the letters once were, as these areas are closer to the original body color, with a slightly darker shade that stands out from the bleached, weathered appearance of the rest of the side. Other prototype photos showed similar effects to varying degrees on other locomotives in this scheme.

I tried to capture this overall look with a factory-painted Atlas HO U33B. My first step was to find a model paint that was close — but not an exact match — to the factory paint on the model. This turned out to be Polly Scale Roof Red. I started by streaking this color across the roof, the cab roof, and down the sides of the locomotive, as seen on the next page.

Seven-year-old Rock Island U33C No. 191 has lost most of its side lettering by the time of this 1976 photo. The bleached, lightened appearance of the paint helps highlight the darker areas where the white lettering has peeled away. Ron Plazzotta

I streaked the roof with a couple of different shades of oxide red paint to simulate paint that was becoming bleached and worn.

I streaked the parts of the lettering that would remain with Roof Red. In hindsight, I should have done this before adding the body weathering.

For the lettering that was gone, I used a fine-tip brush to paint Roof Red over the white factory lettering. It took two coats to completely cover it. It's OK to go over the edges a bit; it won't be noticeable when the model is fully weathered.

This gave a weathered appearance and streaking to the original color.

To create the lettering effect, my original thought was to remove the factory letters, but then I'd have to come up with another way to trace them. I finally figured the best way was to just paint directly over them, as they provided an accurate pattern.

I streaked the Roof Red vertically over the parts of the lettering that remained. I did this by drybrushing the Roof Red across parts of a few letters. I made a mistake here in that I'd applied some weathering to the sides first; it would have been better to wait, and it meant a bit of touch-up later. It's OK if this drybrushed color extends beyond the letters themselves, as it will simply look like weathered streaks.

Next was capturing the look of faded, bleached paint. This would set the stage for the later lettering treatment. I started by applying white chalk into the surface, brushing it firmly with a stiff-bristled brush. I followed with a coat of Krylon clear matte finish; however, some of the effect disappeared. I countered that by giving the sides a light airbrush coat of thinned Polly Scale white, coating the nose, rear, and pilots, as well.

The next step seems daunting, but was easier than I thought it would be. I used the lettering as a template on which to simply brush-paint the Roof Red, using a medium pointed-bristle brush for best control. It takes a fairly steady hand, but going over the edges slightly doesn't affect the final appearance much, as the white background gives the lettering a slightly different shade. It took a couple of coats to completely cover the white and provide an even shade of red, which is important for the final effect.

I finished the model with the same effects applied to other diesels (Chapter 7): brushed grimy black with rust streaks on the fuel tank, followed by an oily black stain below the fuel filler; brushed grimy black on the truck sideframes, followed by dust- and rust-colored powdered chalk and PanPastels on the trucks and tank. The pilot received spot color touch up on the air hoses.

The roof and side radiator grids and grills received washes of black to give them some depth. On the roof, the silver exhaust stack received a wash of grimy black. I next drybrushed grimy black around the stacks and other areas of the roof, then dusted the roof with black powdered chalk, really grinding it in especially around the stack and back on the radiator grids.

A final light overspray of clear flat finish sealed all of the chalk weathering.

NYC BOXCAR

The New York Central boxcar at right is an extreme case of ghost lettering. It started off as a standard 40-foot boxcar in the mid-1940s, then was painted in NYC's distinctive red-and-gray Pacemaker scheme, designed for cars in dedicated merchandise (less-than-carload, or LCL) service. By the 1960s, as railroad LCL traffic moved to trucks and Flexi-Vans, the remaining boxcars in the service reverted to standard service and were repainted to an oxide red scheme.

As you can see, with cars like this it can be difficult to tell which layer is peeling off of which. The old oval herald is showing through where the new one has peeled away, and the road number is impossible to read with elements of both schemes showing through as peeled paint. The gray and red paints are both in multiple shades — you really can't tell which is the bright red Pacemaker color and

I drybrushed and streaked the stack and roof with grimy black to simulate exhaust. It will be followed later with a generous layer of black chalk.

An HO InterMountain boxcar lettered for New York Central was the starting point for this car, based on the prototype car seen at below left. A combination of paint, masking, and dry transfers captured the look of old lettering showing through worn paint.

The weathered New York Central boxcar on the left shows multiple paint schemes, lettering, and heralds showing through peeling layers of paint in this 1974 view. It once wore the bright red-and-gray scheme of the car at right, painted for the railroad's Pacemaker (package) freight service. Note how much the red has faded on the car to the right of the freshly painted car. Left: John Ingles; Right: R.J. Wilhelm

I scraped away much of the reporting marks and number with a hobby knife. Keep the blade flat and work carefully. It's OK if some remnants remain; some of what's left will show through the later paint.

The area under the "Pacemaker" lettering was stippled with light gray. This is the lettering color that will eventually show through.

I applied the dry transfers, burnishing them with just enough pressure to get the lettering to transfer to the body, but not to adhere them securely. The cracked and broken lettering will add to the effect.

the boxcar red, as any remnants of the former have faded severely.

I wanted to re-create this effect in HO scale, and I had as a starting point an InterMountain ready-to-run car in the oxide red scheme. I bought a set of CDS Lettering dry transfers for the Pacemaker scheme (these are out of production, but I easily found a set online), then started planning how to pull it off.

The first tip in modeling a weathered mess of a car like this: Don't sweat your color choices. Things have faded and streaked. You just need to be in the ballpark. Another thing to remember: You want to capture the overall effect, but getting the weathering patterns *exactly* in the right spots isn't necessary. When there are so many variations, patches, and lines, if we're off by a bit, it won't matter unless you're comparing it directly to a prototype photo. What viewers will notice is the car as a whole.

And a third tip: Test any layered, complex techniques and paints on a scrap subject before doing it on the real model. I only had one NYC boxcar on hand, and I didn't want to mess it up. My basic idea was to use masks to layer elements of both paint schemes, then use portions of the dry transfers as a mask to allow underlying color to show through.

I started by removing the trucks. If this were a kit, I would have done all of the painting before adding ladders, stirrups, and grab irons, but as it is, I just tried to be careful and work around them as best as I could.

The first step was to remove much of the original reporting marks and number. I tried a couple of liquid solutions, but it wasn't coming off, so I resorted to a No. 11 blade, using just the edge and holding it as flat to the surface as possible to only remove the lettering and not the underlying paint. The results didn't have to be perfect.

Next was to provide the actual lettering color that would provide the background for the Pacemaker Freight Service lettering, which was a mix of white that had faded to gray, along with some rust and oxide red from the underlying scheme. I did this by stippling some light gray (Polly Scale Undercoat Light Gray) in the area; again, being precise is not needed.

I then applied the dry transfers over that area. I used a very light touch — not enough to firmly burnish the letters to the surface, but just enough to get them to transfer from the backing paper. We need them to be easily removed after the next step in the process. As the photo showed, my light touch resulted in several letters breaking and not completely transferring, which was just fine for this project.

Masking the car was next. I first masked off the lower body (which would be gray) and the entire door. I applied an oval of tape to partially cover the original herald on the right side to match how the underlying herald was partially coming through on the prototype.

I airbrushed the car with oxide red (the color wasn't critical, just so it was somewhere near the model's original color), making sure I covered the areas over the dry transfers and oval. The mask can then be removed.

Pressing masking tape firmly over the dry transfers let me pull them up (it took a couple of repeated efforts to do it), revealing the light gray paint underneath.

I then masked off the top half of the car in preparation for airbrushing the gray. I made an additional mask for the lower half of the car to create the paint-peel pattern of the prototype car. I did this by taking a digital image of the prototype car, straightening out the sides in Photoshop, and printing it out in HO scale. I then taped the printout over masking tape and cut out the overall peel patterns with a hobby knife.

I also added dry transfers for the car number and reporting marks, burnishing them lightly as with the earlier dry transfers. I applied some additional small masked areas with tape and bits of poster putty. The car was then airbrushed Polly Scale Undercoat Light Gray, and the masking and transfers peeled away (see page 91).

The main color work was set, but the car was still far from done. I used a darker shade of gray and brush-painted

Mask the door and bottom of the car. The oval mask simulates the placement of the herald from the paint scheme that has worn away.

After airbrushing with an oxide red color, I removed the dry transfers with masking tape, leaving a mottled effect. The oval mask has also been removed on the right side.

I used a printed copy of the prototype photo as a pattern to cut masks for the peeled paint in the gray area of the car.

PROTOTYPE EXAMPLE: B&O HOPPER BLEED-THROUGH

When the Baltimore & Ohio acquired a series of two-bay hopper cars from Chesapeake & Ohio, the railroad simply painted over the C&O herald and lettering and stenciled its own initials and reporting marks in place. The C&O lettering, however, is readily visible, bleeding through the hastily applied black paint (which is noticeably darker than the car's original weathered, bleached black body paint). A car like this could be re-created in the same way as the real car: apply weathering effects, then use thinned black paint to cover the original herald and lettering, then apply new decals or dry transfers.

Ghost lettering shows through patched-out areas on this Baltimore & Ohio (ex-Chesapeake & Ohio) two-bay hopper, which appears to have been recently restenciled in this February 1962 view. The car was built in the late 1930s. John Ingles

PROTOTYPE EXAMPLE: HIDDEN NP HERALD

Some ghost effects are difficult to spot, or not initially identified as such. It's easy when initially looking at this Northern Pacific boxcar to think that the rust patches forming on the herald are just random, but close examination shows that the circular pattern (at the upper left part of the painted logo) is from the smaller round herald of an earlier paint scheme. You can even see part of the old reverse-S-curve monad pattern (to the right of the O and R) showing through.

The Northern Pacific repainted this boxcar in the early 1960s. Parts of the earlier (smaller) round monad herald are showing through as rust behind the new, larger herald by this 1977 photo. R.J. Wilhelm

wear patterns on the gray of the car, along with grimy weathering streaks. I painted oxide red streaks as well, giving some of the peeled areas a more jagged look.

Medium and dark rust colors were painted in several areas, including along the door sides and tracks and the lower parts of the body near the ends, ladders, and steps. Grimy black accented the placard boards on the door. PanPastels worked well for adding color shades and variations to the red areas of the car.

The car ends received a healthy application of black powdered chalk to match the grime of the prototype car.

The roof and trucks received relatively standard weathering treatments (discussed in Chapter 4). A light coat of clear flat acrylic from an airbrush sealed the weathering effects.

Masking tape cut from the pattern, together with dry-transfer reporting marks/ number and bits of poster putty, covered the areas that will remain red when the gray is applied.

Removing the masks revealed the peeling paint effect. The car is way too clean, however. Now a variety of weathering effects can be applied.

I brush-painted additional shading to both the red and gray areas, and here I'm adding various red shades of PanPastels. I also added rust near the door and on areas of the lettering and ladders, plus additional oxide-red shading of the peeled areas. Some additional grime finished the weathering.

The car ends received a healthy coating of powdered black chalk to represent the grimy ends of the prototype car.

RUSTED-THROUGH LETTERING ON A COVERED HOPPER

Cody Grivno used an HO Accurail three-bay covered hopper to capture ghost lettering from a prototype Santa Fe car he had photographed. The prototype car had been delivered in a red scheme with large road name on the side, with Roman-style reporting marks and number. At some point the car was repainted in a simplified mineral red scheme with Gothic-style reporting marks and a small round herald. As this scheme aged, the paint oxidized and weathered, allowing a rust-colored ghost of the original large side lettering and the old reporting marks to show through.

Cody started with a factory-painted Santa Fe car, airbrushing it with Polly Scale Mineral Red. He made a photocopy of a Microscale decal set for the large-lettering car (No. MC-4346), cutting out the letters to make a stencil for creating the ghost lettering. He airbrushed the car through the stencil with a mix of Polly Scale Rust and Oily Black, thinned to about 50 percent.

When that dried, Cody dusted the car with a mix of Polly Scale Earth, Rust, Oily Black, and Engine Black. The decals for the repainted scheme were applied (Microscale 87-791). Cody finished with thinned Mineral Red over the ghost lettering areas and Polly Scale Clear Flat over the entire car. Two photos: Cody Grivno

BLEED-THROUGH LETTERING ON A SANTA FE BOXCAR

Another example of a Santa Fe car with old lettering appearing through a more-recent scheme is this boxcar. Andy Renshaw did an outstanding job of capturing the look of the old scheme showing through the new.

Andy started with an older Athearn HO boxcar kit, removing its molded-on details, upgrading the door tracks, and removing the running board to match what was done to many prototype boxcars in the late 1960s.

Andy airbrushed dark streaks along the rivet seams and where new details had been added. He also airbrushed the roof silver. He then airbrushed the car with thinned mineral brown, applying light coats until the older lettering was just showing through the paint. He also overcoated the silver roof with red. A coat of clear gloss provided a good base for the new decals.

Andy finished the car with some oil paint weathering on the sides and dust along the lower body. He then scraped some of the red paint from the roof, revealing silver (simulated galvanized) patches. A coat of clear flat finished the project. Three photos: Andy Renshaw

PRECISION IS NOT NEEDED

With ghost and shadow lettering, precise placement isn't necessary — or even desired in many cases. R.G. Hough did a great job of highlighting Soo Line lettering showing through a newer coat of paint on a car sold to the Wisconsin & Southern. He started with an HO Roundhouse model of a PS-2 ballast car and added 3-D printed ballast doors from Circus City Decals (circuscitydecals.com).

After painting the car, he decaled it with a set from Circus City, staggering the lettering a bit. Restenciled cars are often done in a hurry, and exact placement of the new stencils and lettering is sometimes based on factors such as the height of the person doing the work.

The shadow lettering is freehanded. R.G. used a toothpick to add shapes of the lettering with a color slightly lighter than the car, then highlighted small areas of it with dark rust colors. Your eyes and brain connect the dots to know that the lettering once said "Soo Line," even if only part of the faint lettering shows through. He finished the car with some overall grime to further blend the lettering effects into the car side.

The previous owner of this hastily repainted Wisconsin & Southern ballast car is apparent with the shadows of "Soo Line" lettering showing. R.G. Hough

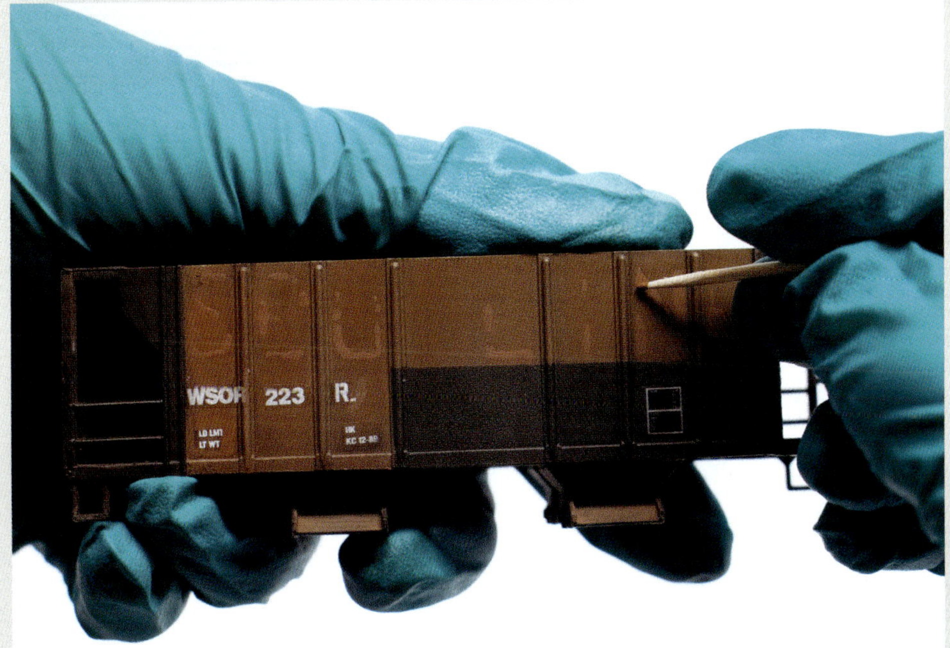

R.G. Hough used a round toothpick to add portions of the Soo letters in a color slightly lighter than the car side. R.G. Hough

CHAPTER TEN

Vehicles show their age in the form of general grime and rust patches. These HO vehicles from Classic Metal Works were weathered using drybrushing, chalks, washes, and rust-paste patches, with some additional spot color and decal details.

Vehicles

Along with the trains themselves, vehicle models go a long way toward setting a layout in a specific era and place. Weathering vehicles can tell a story about their age and the environment they operate in, helping create more realistic scenes.

Looking at this scene today we immediately think, "Classic car!" However, at the time of this 1963 photo, this was simply an older, clean but beat up, auto with significant left-rear damage and rust and a driver's door that doesn't look to be in proper alignment. J. David Ingles

Unlike railroad locomotives and freight cars, automobiles usually receive a lot of tender loving care from their owners — especially when new. Car owners like to wash and wax their babies, keeping them in their clean, like-new appearance for many years.

But once cars are several years old, vehicle care can take a nosedive, with dents and dings, rust, repairs, and damage appearing in various degrees.

If you're modeling a particular year, keep in mind the number of vehicles you have and their ages. For any given period, most cars will be within 5-8 years old; the number of cars for each model year will decline the older you go. There should be fewer older cars, and the older they are, the more weathering they should have.

If you're modeling a rural area or small town in the days before paved roads were common (which is still today in some areas of the West and Midwest), most of your vehicles should have a healthy coating of dust and grime (reflecting the color of gravel used on the roads).

And remember the seasons: Winter and spring in snowy areas will leave autos covered in a dusty grayish-white haze of grime and road salt.

BASIC TECHNIQUES

For starters, add a coat of clear flat or satin finish to vehicles before adding

You can simulate a dirty windshield with wiper marks by masking the appropriate pattern, then applying a flat clear coat. It has also received a light dusting of chalk on the sides, hood, and front.

Replaced parts often appear in the manner of different colors (perhaps the fender on this car came from a junkyard like the one on page 98). Simply paint a panel a different color and add additional weathering (light chalk, in this case).

Missing hubcaps are another common feature, especially on cars through the 1970s. I simply painted a hubcap grimy black and added additional chalk weathering on this HO Classic Metal Works car.

Rust-colored chalk mixed with flat clear finish makes a great paste for simulating heavy rust patches. It provides texture as well as color. Additional chalk can be applied over the still-wet paste. Rust often starts at and around wheel wells and fenders and spreads upward.

them to the layout. Some modelers resist doing this, but remember the reasons given in Chapter 1. Yes, new and freshly washed and waxed prototype vehicles are indeed bright and shiny. But that high-buff sheen does not translate well in scale size and lighting conditions, risking a toy-like appearance. I use a brush to add acrylic flat finish.

From there, you can take weathering to varying levels. I like to use chalks and PanPastels on vehicles, varying the amount of simulated dirt and grime among vehicles and tending to go heavier on older ones. You don't necessarily need to add a clear seal coat, but if the vehicles will be handled frequently, this will avoid fingerprints and smudges.

There are a few specific techniques you can do to make distinctive models. The first is simulating windshield-wiper tracks. You can simply freehand brush flat finish on the windshield if you have a steady hand, or you can cut and apply a basic mask with tape, then apply clear flat around it. For a bit more contrast, brush on some light dust-colored chalk, as well. This will make the effect a bit more apparent.

We've all seen cars that have had panels and hoods replaced with parts from junkyard donors. These are, on older vehicles, often left in their original colors — for example, a blue car with a red front fender, as seen at top left. This is easy to simulate by brush-painting a panel or hood a different color. Similarly, painting a fender or quarter panel primer red or gray can simulate a body part that's been repaired, but not repainted.

Another related feature is a missing hubcap or wheel cover, a common detail on older cars. Depending upon the model involved, you can sometimes simply paint the existing hubcap or cover dark gray or brown. You may be able to pry off the original hubcap — again, it depends on the model manufacturer and level of detail of the car.

For older, weatherbeaten vehicles, the telltale sign of age is rust. This can be minor patches or large areas. Rust commonly starts next to the wheel wells and along the lower sides (espe-

Along with rust-paste areas, the finished Dodge (from CMW) also has drybrushed rust streaks, grime and rust washes on the grill, a couple of body scrapes painted with rust colors, and a light dusting of chalk.

cially in the north, where salt is used in the winter) and grows from there. Rust can also start in dings and dents.

I model this with a chalk paste made by mixing rust-colored powdered chalk into a drop of clear flat finish or matte medium. The paste is then brushed in place or applied with a toothpick. This adds texture along with the color, providing a 3-D appearance that paint alone doesn't provide.

Additional weathering can be applied with any of the common techniques: drybrushing for rust, along with washes, chalks, or PanPastels for general grime. Oil paints also work well for rust effects.

TRUCKS

Trucks can be given similar treatment. The amount of dirt and grime on a truck depends upon its owner and use. A private owner — say an owner-operator of a semi or local delivery truck — will likely keep his vehicle in clean, nice condition. Trucks that are part of larger fleets will vary; some are kept fairly clean to give a good image of the brands represented by their paint

Most general-service trucks have enameled or painted grills, not chrome, so I painted this grill white. I followed it with a wash of black for depth; the finished results can be seen in the photo on page 94.

JUNKYARD: EXTREME VEHICLE WEATHERING

You can take weathering to an extreme to create realistic depictions of scrapped and abandoned cars. The resulting hulks can be placed in a junkyard scene such as this or in vacant lots, back alleys, and backyards. Small junkyards are often visible from roads and railroad rights-of-way. They can also be the centerpieces of a larger rail-served scrapyard.

These vehicles are the work of Horst Meier and his son Markus. Horst explains that this is a great use for toy vehicles, models with damage, and those with detailing that simply no longer stands up to your current standards of realism.

They start by removing parts including doors, hoods, and tailgates, simulating parts that have been removed and sold. Horst and Markus also inflict damage on bodies to simulate wreck damage (dents) and exposure to the elements (holes that have "rusted through" bodies). This can be done with a motor tool, razor saw, or hobby knife. Wheels can be removed; they make many tires "flat" by sanding or filing them flat on the bottom side.

Models then receive coats of rust-colored paints, followed by applications of rust-colored chalks and powdered pastels, which help add texture.

The junkyard scene was further accented by stacking parts among the vehicles and adding significant weed and plant growth to show that some have been there for a long time. You can see more of Horst and Markus' work in the November 2011 issue of *Model Railroader*.

Photos: Horst and Markus Meier

Washes can be effective on many textured surfaces on trucks, especially trailers with vertical-post or beaded/corrugated sides. This is a thinned black acrylic wash, just heavy enough to add some contrast.

schemes, but other companies rarely gave their trucks and trailers a washing.

As with autos, a good first step is brushing on a coat of clear flat finish. Paint the underframe, including the interior wheel wells and chassis, flat black. (These areas on truck models are often painted or molded in the body color, which jumps out as unrealistic).

Grills and front bumpers on model trucks are often chromed. In real life, most trucks — especially delivery-type trucks and those in fleet service — have grills and bumpers painted white, off-white, or to match the body color. Chrome on trucks is usually reserved for semis operated by private owners.

Use a brush to paint these areas. I used flat white on the Sunshine truck on page 97, followed by a black wash (I prefer flat black craft paint thinned with water). Make sure the grill is as level as possible to keep the wash from flowing out of the gaps. When that dries, you can add a second wash if it's not dark enough. Clean up any grill areas as needed.

I like to add a few detail decals to trucks and trailers, such as license plates and marker lights (Microscale makes great sets for this: MC-4168 [HO] and 60-4168 [N]). I added a cab-door sign to the Sunshine truck (a logo I found online and printed out) as well as decal numbers to indicate it was part of a fleet.

Truck wheels are sometimes painted to match the body color and are sometimes black. They become grimy quickly, so a wash of black or grimy black will both dirty them a bit and add contrast, enabling you to see details better. Tires start out black, but become lighter as they age. You can capture this with shades of dark gray to grimy black, depending upon the age.

Trucks also have parts that can be highlighted, such as door details (hinges, latch bars, handle) with gray or rust-color artist's pencils (in much the same way as a freight car). The landing gear, mud flaps, and any visible parts of the suspension can be given a coat of grime or rust.

Van trailers, especially through the 1960s when pollution controls weren't as stringent, often acquired a dark soot pattern on their upper front corners from the exhaust stack of diesel tractors. This is most common on the upper right side, but can be found on the left as well (early truck tractors most often had single stacks on the right, with others having dual stacks).

Truck bodies can receive overall general grime, dust, and dirt with the usual methods. The basic goal is to make it look like the truck works hard for a living.

Wheels are often painted black, gray, or the body color (they're rarely chrome on trailers). A thinned black wash simulates grime and adds depth and contrast, making details stand out.

Older trailers often had exhaust stains on the upper front corners. This is easy to replicate with black or dark gray powdered chalk and a soft brush.

CHAPTER ELEVEN

Structures, bridges, and details

Other than the locomotives and freight cars themselves, structures and bridges make the biggest visual impact on a layout. Their sheer size often makes them even more prominent, especially if they tower above the trains or dominate scenes.

Because of this, structures — along with other details such as fences, roads, retaining walls, and the track itself — all deserve care in their paint and weathering treatment. The key with any of these items is being able to capture the look of their materials, such as brick, wood, corrugated steel, and concrete, to achieve realism. The number of possibilities involved preclude delving into great detail in a single chapter, but I recommend expert modeler Lance Mindheim's book *How to Build Structures* (Kalmbach, 2024) for a detailed look at techniques.

Some of these models and materials require specialized techniques, but many can be weathered with the same techniques and materials used throughout this book.

We'll look at a few basic ways to realistically weather structures, bridges, and details, but keep two basic things in mind:

• Unpainted plastic looks like plastic, regardless of the color in which it's molded. Plastic components can nicely capture the texture of many materials, but it absolutely needs to be painted and weathered to kill the plastic shine. Ignore the "molded in realistic colors"

Cody Grivno modeled this HO model of a weather-worn, disused Northern Pacific depot starting with an American Model Builders laser-cut wood kit. He used a variety of techniques to simulate worn and peeling paint. Cody also removed and shifted random shingles (exposing bare subroof in places), painted some shingles different colors, drybrushed light gray streaks on the roof, and added airbrushed soot effects near the chimney. Broken windows (cut and scribed clear plastic) finish the effect. Firecrown Media

marketing slogans on kits and models.

• Structure colors should be subdued and subtle. The vast majority of structures tend to be white, gray, tan, or a shade of brick red or oxide red. Bright colors will stand out — usually not in a good way. Weathering helps tie all of this together.

As with locomotives and rolling stock, the age of structures is often revealed through how much they have weathered. The older the building, the heavier the weathering. And remember that any structure near the tracks in the steam era will have acquired a serious layer of soot from exposure to passing steam locomotives.

BRICK

Brick is among the most common building materials for structures, especially for industrial buildings and storefronts that typically stood near the tracks into the early diesel era. The first step for brick is to provide a good base for weathering by painting the structure an appropriate base color. Prototype brick varies widely in color, so any shade from medium to dark red and various shades of red-brown and dark brown will work. Tan brick is seen in the Midwest. Whatever color you use, make sure the sheen is flat.

Adding mortar detail can be done in several ways. My favorite is with an acrylic wash, bottom right. For color, mortar can range from light gray (it's rarely white) to dark gray, and often is shaded toward the brick color. A good starting point is light gray with a few drops of white and a few drops of an oxide red color to get a light grayish red. Mix this with about 80% to 90% thinner (in my case, windshield-washer solution); water will cause the wash to bead up on the surface.

With the building wall lying flat, use a wide, flat, soft brush to apply the wash. It will flow readily along and through the mortar lines, settling into the depressions. Be aware that it will also tint the brick surface, so the brick color will usually end up lighter than the red that you started with. (Here's a good example of why you should test the effect before applying it to a finished structure.) Let the wash dry thoroughly.

You can follow the mortar wash with any number of additional weathering effects, including drybrushing, washes, chalks, or oversprays. The building at the top of page 104 shows the effects of adding two types of thinned black washes over the mortar effects. Check prototype photos (or real buildings) for ideas.

You can also use powdered chalk to represent mortar (see page 104). Start with light to medium gray chalk, and mix in dark red until you get the color desired. Use a soft brush to spread it across the surface. You can wipe it off the surface using a soft cloth or paper towel. Seal it with a light coat of clear flat (the effect will usually diminish once the clear coat is applied).

An effective detail technique is to paint individual bricks in different colors, something found on many prototype structures. You can use a brush with paint or artist's pencils in various colors.

WOOD EFFECTS

Kits and assembled buildings and details that have simulated wood components — clapboard, board-and-batten siding, planks, wood decks — can be either molded plastic or actual

Mortar colors vary; start with light to medium gray acrylic paint with a few drops of the brick color, then thin the mix with about 90 percent windshield washer fluid. Test and adjust the color before applying it to a large area. Use a wide, flat brush; make sure the walls lay flat so the mortar flows evenly.

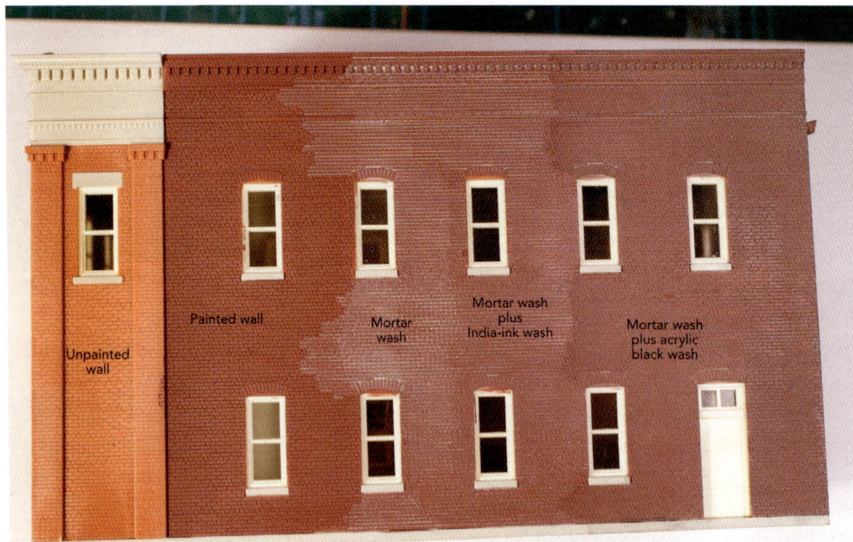

This wall of an injection-molded plastic HO Walthers brick structure kit shows a progression from left: unpainted plastic wall; painted wall; mortar wash added; mortar wash plus thinned India-ink wash; and mortar wash plus thinned acrylic black wash. Some individual bricks have been painted at far right.

Powdered chalk also works well for simulating mortar and weathered, oxidized brick. Use a soft brush to distribute it; wipe the brick faces with a paper towel to concentrate the chalk in the mortar lines. The sign is a homemade decal.

wood. The basics of how to treat and weather these materials to simulate wood is covered in Chapter 6, using flatcar decks as examples.

To model wood components that have been painted, the treatment is the same. Paint the part, then weather it as needed with chalks, washes, and drybrushing. A light, thin wash of grimy black or black will often help bring out detail, providing depth and creating shadow highlights.

A common goal with wood structures is simulating the look of fading, peeling paint, often showing underlying weathered wood. With real wood pieces, the basic method is to stain the wood, paint it the desired color, then remove and damage some of the finish coat to reveal the underlying weathered wood.

A common method that has been used for decades to simulate peeling paint — because it's easy and effective — is the rubber-cement technique seen at right. Stain the wood the desired weathered color (thinned black or gray flat acrylic paint, India ink in alcohol, or actual wood stain are common choices). When that dries, dab small amounts of rubber cement on the surface, making sure to keep the dabs on individual boards. The effect can be as minimal or extensive as you desire.

Paint the model the finish color with an airbrush or brush. When the finish coat is dry, remove the rubber cement to reveal the underlying weathered wood. You can use a knife blade

Brush-paint individual bricks with various red-brown colors. You can also use artist's pencils to highlight bricks.

To simulate peeling paint, apply small dabs of rubber cement to stained wood, as Cody Grivno is doing to an HO laser-cut structure (left). After painting the finish colors, Cody is removing the cement (here using a hobby knife) to reveal the weathered wood beneath the color (right). Two photos: Bill Zuback

or an artist's gum eraser to remove the cement (avoid pink erasers, as they tend to leave undesired color behind).

Another method to achieve a more fine, detailed effect, is to use a wire brush to distress and remove the paint coat. Stain the wood as before, then give the walls a thin coat of the finish color. Using a small wire brush (Micro-Mark's Distresser tool works well), scrape the painted surface, following the grain of the wood (along the lines of the clapboard or vertically with board-and-batten walls).

Yet another technique is to limit the overlying paint coat. To do this, stain the wood as before. Apply the final color with a drybrush technique, wiping off most of the paint on the brush and swiping it along the boards. This is great for situations like the fence shown on page 106, where you want minimal color still clinging to heavily weathered wood.

Wood is sometimes left unpainted. This is common for trestles, retaining walls, loading docks, line poles, and similar structures. In this case, the wood is almost always treated with creosote or other preservative.

To simulate this, you can simply stain the wood with medium to dark grays, black, or medium to dark browns to achieve the desired color. Treated wood generally starts out dark (sometimes nearly black) and fades to lighter gray over the years. Again, check prototype examples and photos for appropriate colors.

Stain wood pieces that will be glued together before assembly; stray glue on the wood surface will prevent it from taking stain.

BRIDGES

Bridges come in many styles and sizes. Most modern bridges are steel, initially painted either black or silver. These tend to weather as freight cars do, with vertical streaks of grime and eventual rust patches and streaks. The same techniques can thus be used.

I used a variation of this to model a silver-painted bridge that has begun to weather with rusted streaks. I started by painting the bridge dark brown with streaks of lighter rust colors. I then airbrushed silver in vertical streaks over the rust colors. This technique will also work with drybrushing and washes.

Here Cody demonstrates another way to model peeling paint, with Micro-Mark's Distresser, a brush with stiff steel bristles. Weather the wood and apply a thin finish coat. Scrub the Distresser with the grain (left), removing as much paint as desired (middle). A wood finishing pad (right) removes fuzz raised by the Distresser. Three photos: Cody Grivno

On this HO scale laser-cut wood fence from Bar Mills, I started by staining the wood with thinned black acrylic paint (right). I followed by drybrushing an oxide-red acrylic over the stained paint (above) to create a varied effect, simulating a weather-worn fence that still retained some color.

Exposed wood components, such as this wood trestle, are generally treated lumber. This is typically dark brown to near black when new, fading to light gray with age. I started with a medium gray stain on these trestle components, streaking several with dark brown and dark gray washes and drybrushing.

The bridge abutments in those photos provide a good illustration of painting and weathering concrete. New concrete tends to be a uniform light gray (almost white). Over years of exposure to the elements, it turns darker as fine grains are washed away, revealing more of the color of the aggregates within, shifting toward a tan tint.

Concrete is also porous, so it stains easily. This is especially noticeable wherever steel components rest on it or are connected to it. Bridge pedestals rust, leaving reddish to dark-brown streaks down abutments. This is easily captured with drybrushing, washes, and powders.

STREETS AND HIGHWAYS

Roadways on model railroads often don't get the attention to weathering detail they deserve. Many modelers simply paint asphalt highways black or dark gray and concrete streets light gray (or "concrete" model paint) and leave it at that.

However, if you look carefully at any street or road, you'll see a wide range of colors depending upon its material, which can vary based on the color of local aggregates. Whether asphalt or concrete, the overall color is made up of thousands of small pebbles and particles that make up its surface, each of which varies in color, along with effects from wear.

Other factors include age and amount of traffic. Traffic lanes from vehicle wear are usually quite visible, along with stains from oil, other vehicle fluid leaks, and tire marks. Repairs are also readily apparent in the form of asphalt or fresh concrete patches or cracks that have been repaired with tar.

To model a roadway, start with the base color. For asphalt, this can be any light to dark gray, depending upon the intended age of the road (the older it is, the lighter it gets). For concrete, I usually start with a model concrete color mixed with white — again, adjusting based on age, but turning darker as it ages. In either case, make sure the paint is flat.

A black or dark gray wash can be effective and add some color variation. Use a wide sponge brush and make

Tony Koester painted this HO steel plate-girder bridge black and weathered it with powders. The concrete abutment is balsa, covered with a wash of plaster. Tony painted it Polly Scale Sand and weathered it with powders. The pilings and retaining walls at right are styrene painted dark brown and weathered with powders to simulate wood. Tony Koester

I painted this HO steel bridge in reverse, starting with dark and medium brown rust colors and overspraying it with light coats of silver, letting some base color show through. I then added the decal logo and drybrushed of rust colors. Note also the rust streaks down the concrete abutment.

This rural Midwestern road shows the many color shades typical of asphalt highways, including the tire paths and wear along with various fluid stains and tar repairs. Note how the road in the foreground is much lighter than the newer pavement in the distance. J. David Ingles

STREAKED, PEELING PAINT

Russ Watson did a masterful job of creating a vertical peeled-paint effect on this scratchbuilt wood handcar shed on his On30 layout. After staining the wood, he rubbed a sanding stick over it vertically to create a varied effect. Russ then dipped a Microbrush into artist's oil paint, rubbed it on a paper towel to remove most of the paint, and applied paint to each board — more at the top than the bottom. He then used a finger to spread the paint downward, creating a realistic, streaked effect. He notes that if the effect is too heavy, you can use a sanding stick to remove it and redo it.

sure the wash doesn't pool, which can leave unrealistic marks and patterns.

The dark trails from traffic are distinctive. Whether the dark trail is the area driven on by tires or the area between the tires depends on the road surface material, color, and age; look at prototype examples and photos. Duplicating this effect can be done with black or dark gray powdered chalk by streaking it along the road surface. Use as large a brush as possible for the smoothest effect. You can also use your fingers to smooth this and further spread and feather the chalk.

An airbrush also works well — use a thin mix (about 5-10% black paint in thinner). You can freehand it along the road or you can use a template or jig to help keep the effect exactly where you need it.

You can then add details: pavement cracks with an artist's pencil, tar patches with a brush or paint marker, and oil and fluid stains and tire marks with a brush (directly painted or drybrushed). A nice example of a finished street is shown on page 110.

A black acrylic paint/alcohol wash, here applied to a sidewalk, brings out detail in expansion joints and cracks and highlights surface texture.

CORRUGATED-METAL STRUCTURES

Many industrial buildings, such as this mine headhouse, were built with corrugated steel panels. Accurately coloring and weathering the galvanized surface of these can be a challenge. Jim Kelly did it on this injection-molded plastic HO scale Walthers model by scribing marks to separate the individual panels (three- to four-foot widths and an eight-foot length are common).

After giving the walls a coat of Polly Scale Reefer Gray (any light, flat gray will work), Jim effectively highlighted the separation between rows of panels by placing masking tape at the top of the scribed panel line, then drybrushing acrylic rust colors downward in streaks. Removing the mask reveals a well-defined edge between rows. After finishing a row, simply move down to the next, also adding some rust highlights between panels.

Jim gave the entire structure a light airbrush coat of thinned earth colors to blend the effects.

Jim Kelly painted and weathered this Walthers coal loader for a *Model Railroader* project layout. The weathering highlights the corrugated-metal surface and the simulated seams between wall panels. Firecrown Media

Jim masked the top edge of a row of panels, then drybrushed rust-colored streaks downward. He then repeated the process, starting at the top of each wall. Firecrown Media

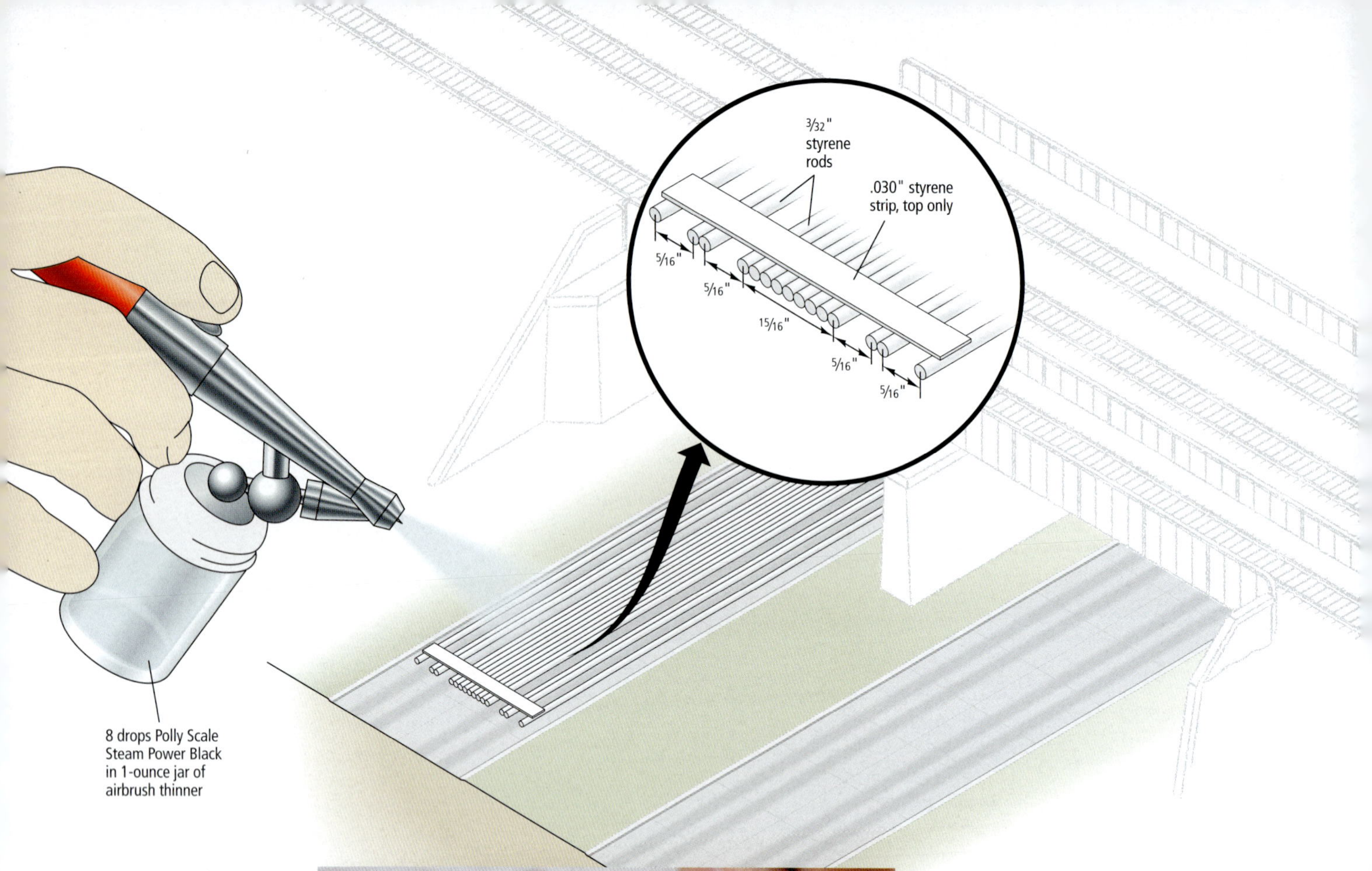

3/32" styrene rods

.030" styrene strip, top only

5/16"

5/16"

15/16"

5/16"

5/16"

8 drops Polly Scale Steam Power Black in 1-ounce jar of airbrush thinner

Above: An airbrush works well for creating road wear. Cody Grivno built a masking jig based on this drawing; the rounded edges of the dowels will provide a soft, feathered edge for the thinned airbrushed paint.

Left: Powdered chalk works well for creating lane-wear details. Here I'm using black chalk to simulate tire wear along a lane used by a rubber-tired container loader at an N scale intermodal yard.

Bottom left: Howard Clark uses poured plaster for streets on his HO layout. After carving expansion joints, bricks, and cracks, he paints it with Woodland Scenics concrete paint and gives it an India ink/alcohol wash, which tints it and highlights the cracks and texture. He then adds further washes to simulate traffic wear. Lou Sassi

Below: Cracks can be drawn on roads with black artist's pencil; black paint markers work well for simulating where cracks have been patched with tar. The lane wear was created with black powdered chalk, streaked by a soft brush.

WEATHERING TRACK

The track itself is another feature that's too often overlooked by modelers. Today's flextrack and turnouts generally offer very nice features in terms of fine spike and tie-plate detail and wood grain on ties. However, the shiny sides of the rail and glossy sheen of molded ties leave a lot to be desired.

Simply painting the entire track assembly a flat dark brown goes a long way to improving appearance. This is easiest done with an airbrush or spray can (use only with adequate ventilation), but can be done with a brush, as well.

Paint markers work well for painting the rail itself; I like to do this with multiple rust colors. Testor's — and earlier, Floquil — have offered markers in several rust and weathering colors. Brush-painting also works.

When moving the markers along the rail, the spikes and tie plates will also pick up some rust-color paint, which is effective.

You can then paint individual ties with washes of medium and light gray and black, as Paul Dolkos is doing in the photo at bottom right. Again, adjust the color to indicate the age of the track. Older ties weather to lighter gray; new treated ties are dark brown to nearly black.

Be sure to clean the railheads with a track-cleaning block as soon as the paint dries.

Effective weathering on track includes flat, varied coloring on ties; rust in various shades on the rail sides and base; and rust along the tie plates and spikes.

Paint markers do a good, quick job of adding rust color to the rails. I like to use two or three shades of brown and rust, layering and streaking them.

Individual ties can be brush-painted various shades of gray and brown, as Paul Dolkos is doing here. Paul Dolkos